CLAIM YOUR WORTH NOW

CLAIM YOUR WORTH NOW

WORTHY WEEKLY INSPIRATION

TODDCHELLE YOUNG

NEW DEGREE PRESS

COPYRIGHT © 2021 TODDCHELLE YOUNG

All rights reserved.

CLAIM YOUR WORTH NOW

Worthy Weekly Inspiration

ISBN	978-1-63730-452-5	*Paperback*
	978-1-63730-561-4	*Kindle Ebook*
	978-1-63730-562-1	*Ebook*

*To the curious, loud, and unrelenting kids in New Haven, CT,
Your dreams are possible. Keep reaching higher and asking for more.*

CONTENTS

	INTRODUCTION	11
WEEK 1.	YOU CAN START OVER	19
WEEK 2.	REMEMBER YOUR WHY	25
WEEK 3.	DO YOU MAKE SENSE TO YOU?	29
WEEK 4.	EXCUSES DON'T GET RESULTS	33
WEEK 5.	LET IT GO	39
WEEK 6.	THIS, TOO, SHALL PASS	43
WEEK 7.	THE STRUGGLE MAKES YOU STRONGER	47
WEEK 8.	OLD WAYS WON'T OPEN NEW DOORS	53
WEEK 9.	WE REPEAT WHAT WE DON'T REPAIR	57
WEEK 10.	LISTEN TO YOUR DREAM	61
WEEK 11.	COMMIT ON PURPOSE	65
WEEK 12.	THE HUSTLE IS SOLD SEPARATELY	69
WEEK 13.	A PASS FORWARD	73
WEEK 14.	PAY YOURSELF FIRST	77
WEEK 15.	YES TO NEW FRIENDS	81
WEEK 16.	DOING WHAT'S MOST DIFFICULT	85
WEEK 17.	WHO SAID YOU COULDN'T?	89
WEEK 18.	CONNECT WITH YOURSELF	95
WEEK 19.	DON'T LET THE INTERNET RUSH YOU	99
WEEK 20.	RECLAIM YOUR TIME	103
WEEK 21.	BREATHE IN, BREATHE OUT	107
WEEK 22.	SAY NO	111
WEEK 23.	ASK THE QUESTION	115
WEEK 24.	ELIMINATE WHAT DOESN'T HELP YOU EVOLVE	119
WEEK 25.	YOU MATTER MORE	123

WEEK 26.	TAKE THE DAY OFF	127
WEEK 27.	BE FLEXIBLE	131
WEEK 28.	CHECK YOUR PRIORITIES	135
WEEK 29.	DREAM REAL BIG	139
WEEK 30.	CHOOSE ACTION OVER ANGER	143
WEEK 31.	STICK TO YOUR PLAN	147
WEEK 32.	SURROUND YOURSELF WITH GREAT PEOPLE	151
WEEK 33.	IT'S OK TO CRY	155
WEEK 34.	PLAN ACCORDINGLY	159
WEEK 35.	LEAN INTO YOUR IDENTITIES	163
WEEK 36.	WRITE OUT THE VISION	167
WEEK 37.	BEYOND THE STATUS QUO	173
WEEK 38.	MIND YOUR BUSINESS	177
WEEK 39.	TO KNOW OR NOT TO KNOW	181
WEEK 40.	MAKE YOUR ___ HEALTH PRIORITY	185
WEEK 41.	CLAP FOR YOURSELF	189
WEEK 42.	MORE MONEY, NEW OPPORTUNITIES	193
WEEK 43.	STICK TO THE BASICS	197
WEEK 44.	THE TIDE IS TURNING	201
WEEK 45.	YOUR MOMENT IS NOW	205
WEEK 46.	THE JOURNEY HAS JUST BEGUN	209
WEEK 47.	SEASONS GREETINGS	213
WEEK 48.	EVERYTHING THAT GLITTERS	219
WEEK 49.	PERSISTENCE IS KEY	223
WEEK 50.	GO WHERE OTHERS WILL NOT	227
WEEK 51.	PISS THEM OFF	231
WEEK 52.	LET'S WIN, TOGETHER	235

CONCLUSION	239
ACKNOWLEDGMENTS	243
APPENDIX	247

"You can only become truly accomplished at something you love. Don't make money your goal. Instead, pursue the things you love doing, and then do them so well that people can't take their eyes off you."

—MAYA ANGELOU

INTRODUCTION

When I was twelve years old, I found myself at a crossroads: Be what everyone around me expected me to be or be unapologetically myself. I opted for the former just so I could share mutual experiences with others in the neighborhood, yet I had no idea of the impact those actions would have on my future identity.

I was known as the "smart one," met with my four-foot, nine-inch self and deliberate use of the English language defining my perceived innocence. Though I tried to uphold everyone's expectations of me, I also noticed my reasoning, goals, and preferences were different from many of my peers.

Unlike other kids my age, I was not moved by the latest fashion trends or shiny new gadgets. I was moved by books, imagining my life like those I read about and someday living a life outside of poverty.

During the summers of 2002 and 2003, I crossed the road that would change my perspective on life as a young woman. I came into womanhood unannounced, and that came with sudden unexpected stares and interests. Growing up in housing projects didn't shield me and my peers from "grown-up realities." Many of us were expected to begin working to help raise siblings or even raise children—yes, at twelve years old.

Everyday stresses wore on me, and I was forced to comprehend what all of it meant—how I would choose to exist in this space. Grappling with big concepts like faith, sexuality, love, support, and success was exhausting. Amid it all, uncertainty about where life would take me was a constant irritant.

Until, one day, when I'd had enough of my realities, I made a clear and uncompromising promise to myself. Regardless of what life would throw at me now and in the future, I would never stop learning, always do my best, be compassionate, and never give up on the life I imagined.

COMMITTING TO THE DREAM
Motivation can come from anywhere: a book, a catchy saying, a pretty picture, or even a hole in the ground.

For Dr. Tererai Trent, a renowned scholar, author, and humanitarian, her story began in her small village in Zimbabwe, where women struggled to receive an education.

In an interview with Marie Forleo, host of MarieTV on YouTube, Dr. Trent recalled the war that liberated Zimbabwe when the country opened its borders to foreigners, after the Rhodesian Bush War ended in 1979. (MarieTV, 2019)

Dr. Trent met American and Australian women who were likely in Zimbabwe to aid with post-war recovery and peace-keeping efforts. Dr. Trent talked about admiring the American and Australian women's "sense of empowerment" and how they "loved themselves." (MarieTV, 2019)

One particular American woman asked Dr. Trent and a group of women from the village a question Dr. Trent has never forgotten: "What are your dreams?"

Though silent at first and hesitant to answer, after being nudged Dr. Trent responded her dream was to receive an undergraduate degree, master's degree, and PhD in America.

The other women were perplexed and looked at her like she was crazy, especially since she did not even have a high school diploma at that time.

Customarily, *dreams* were not meant for women in her village; women's sole purpose was to raise children.

Dr. Trent was conditioned to believe that she was nothing, though she had dreams and goals. She had much to deal with as an abused woman, a wife, and a twenty-two year old with four children. But whether it was the nudge by the American woman or the foreigners' self-empowerment, Dr. Trent was inspired to no longer hold on to the "baton of poverty" passed from her ancestors.

Dr. Trent returned home and shared this experience with her mother, who told her to go out and conquer her dreams. Dr. Trent said that her mother's blessing "was her inheritance."

"Write down your dreams and bury them in the same way we bury the umbilical cord," her mother had proclaimed.

Dr. Trent's village believes when the umbilical cord is buried, wherever the child goes, they will always remember where they come from and be reminded of their importance. Motivated by her mother's encouragement, Dr. Trent wrote out her four dreams and showed them to her mother.

"I see you only have four dreams—personal dreams," her mother responded. "I want you to remember this: Your dreams in this life will have greater meaning when they are tied to the betterment of your community."

With this in mind, Dr. Trent wrote down a fifth dream: Return to Zimbabwe to improve the lives of women and girls by helping them gain access to education. She folded up her paper and buried her dreams in a tin can in the yard, thus beginning her journey.

YOUR OWN JOURNEY
So many people seem to believe long-term goals are just difficult, but there are other reasons such as health conditions, financial matters, and family responsibilities that lead to burying dreams and forgetting about them.

When Dr. Trent was told to bury her dreams, she realized it wasn't about burying the dreams but remembering her goals might take longer than she thought.

This practice does not have to be unique to Dr. Trent. "Burying your dreams" is the first step to intentional goal setting.

Our lived experiences and the life we desire do not have to be at odds. Even when we set goals, admiring the lives of others makes us feel as if we haven't achieved our dreams quickly enough. The pursuit of our dreams and its ups and downs are met with anxiety, stress, and depression.

According to Market Research, the total US self-improvement market was worth $9.9 billion in 2016, with the need for resources in times of uncertainty increasing tenfold annually—not to mention the desire for instant gratification. (LaRosa, 2018)

Further, many people believe inspiration has to be structured, habitual, or that you have to find a person who you should model your life after, but this isn't necessarily true. Yes, you can get inspiration from someone, but everyone has their own journey and paths forward to accomplishing their goals.

For Dr. Trent, she buried her dreams and had the internal fire to accomplish them—it took her almost ten years to earn a high school diploma. Afterward, she received a scholarship to complete her bachelor's degree in the United States, journeying across the Atlantic with her five children and husband in tow.

To say that balancing college with family responsibilities was a struggle would be a gross understatement. In those early college years, Dr. Trent felt like she was doing a disservice to her children by spending most of her time pursuing her dreams instead of focusing entirely on them.

Her family struggled financially, and her marriage suffered. Dr. Trent's situation at home became so difficult she had to ask for cafeteria food leftovers at her university and would often retrieve them from the garbage.

There were days when she wanted to give up on her dreams, and if she had, it would have been justified. But she continued to move forward. In a span of twenty years, not only did she finish her bachelor's degree, she completed two masters' degrees and her PhD, and she also started a nonprofit to help women and girls in Zimbabwe.

Dr. Trent's story caught the attention of Oprah Winfrey. Oprah was so moved by Dr. Trent's story she invested in Tererai's dream— she donated $1.5 million to help Dr. Trent rebuild the dilapidated school in her village in Zimbabwe along with a three-year commitment to have educators present.

Every step of the way, through immeasurable odds, Dr. Tererai pushed through her obstacles.

THE QUESTION IS, CAN WE?
I believe that we can accomplish our dreams, even when they seem frighteningly big or impossible. Similar to Dr. Trent, I believe our inspiration to realize our dreams needs to be intentional. Intentionality does not mean the journey will be easy. This also doesn't mean that the journey

ahead will look like someone else's. You must know exactly what you are reaching for. A bump in the road doesn't mean that the dream is over, or your inspiration is not working—I am pretty sure it is working—you just have to keep your eyes on the prize and be relentless about getting the reward.

Each week can be a bit much. Whether it is completing a project or assignment, child rearing, or balancing both of these and more. By mid-week, I am exhausted, as many of us are.

By Wednesday, my mind starts to wonder about everything that must be wrapped up by Friday, *and* how I can be doing my life better. *Then*, I have to find enough energy and motivation to be productive for the rest of the week.

The weekend can be a breath of fresh air and freedom for some, but for others it is a hard sigh and a long list of overdue tasks. *Which are you?*

I am convinced everyone needs a mid-week jumpstart into a successful weekend. From planning your brunch budget to long-term goals, Wednesday is a good day to realign your goals so you can conquer them all.

Intentional inspiration is understanding how today's happiest and most successful people use the power of intention and purpose to drive their lives forward. From Dr. Trent to Malala Yousafzai to Steve Jobs, life's circumstances and passions propel you forward into the life you desire.

If you need an additional "-umph" *or* you know exactly what you want but it has been difficult to remain inspired, to get motivated, and to commit to moving yourself forward, this is the book for you!

It is on this very day when you need a word or something to lift your spirits to propel you toward your day "off" or the weekend. *Claim Your Worth Now* covers intentional inspiration, momentary reflection, and purposeful action.

I was compelled to write *Claim Your Worth Now* to share my story of ups and downs, as well as stories from other successful people to provide a framework of how to fight for success when the odds don't seem to be in your favor. I am interested in understanding how people find inspiration to move forward and *actually* conquer their dreams. I believe my lived experiences and lessons from experts align with what I will communicate to you over the next fifty-two weeks. I, too, come from a place where dreams were not only deferred, but derailed and defunct. But week by week, we can build toward the future we deserve.

Now let's get your dreams accomplished!

WEEK 1

YOU CAN START OVER

"I have not failed. I've just found 10,000 ways that won't work."
—THOMAS A. EDISON

Imagine what can happen if you channel your fear, denial, and thoughts into a step forward? That's a lot of energy going into one step!

Everyone has been in situations where they haven't lived up to expectations. Personally, there have been moments when I completely screwed things up like forgetting to pay rent. One time the eviction warning was taped to the front door, but the most memorable was receiving my transcript at the end of my first year in college stating I was on academic probation.

Though I worked really hard, everything happening in my life made being successful seem impossible. I honestly felt like there weren't any reasons to continue trying, and I should drop out to work for my family's sake. Thoughts like these would replay themselves, beating me up emotionally until I was imagining myself not accomplishing my goal of graduating college at all.

It was devastating!

I was not willing to let success sail by me and live unfulfilled, so I knew I had to compete with the thought distortions in my head. Eventually, I found the strength within myself to suck it up and try college again, and then again.

The "buy-in principle of commitment," developed by Rory Vaden in *Take the Stairs: 7 Steps to Achieving True Success*, states that the more we have invested into something, the less likely we are to let it fail. (Vaden, 2013)

I had invested time, others invested financially toward my tuition, and I refused to let my dream fail. The motivation ultimately came from reminding myself why I started out on my journey in the first place.

My "why" required clear defining, and this demanded tough and necessary questions:

Why am I here?

What am I living for?

What encourages me to give back and want to serve?

How can I make this dream possible?

Do I have resources, tools, experiences, and opportunities to enable me to do all I am asking for and want to do?

Asking myself these questions was *the* game-changer. When I discovered the answer was *no* to this last question, I knew I didn't have a choice but to figure out what I actually needed to do.

My particular struggle was my journey to medical school. It certainly wasn't, and still isn't, a walk in the park. As a first-generation college graduate, parent to my youngest brother, and full-time employee to provide for my family, moving forward with my journey was a decision I made that ended up requiring grit and sacrifice.

While I did not have pressure from my family to pursue this career choice, as many people do, my calling to this profession made matters even more frustrating.

Frustration and difficulties along the way are usually reasons why people decide that the choice they made is not for them.

This is not a reason to give up and certainly not a reason to throw the entire dream away.

The struggle right now may be real, but if your "why" is strong and clear enough to keep the fire in you lit, your decision to move forward, even if you must start over, is the right one.

When you understand why your initial path didn't work out well the first time, you can navigate your course with the necessary adjustments.

The "traditional" path isn't for everyone.

If you want something bad enough and you can't imagine life without it, the number of tries doesn't matter; what matters is that one time when you succeed. That one success will be the launching pad to the next, and the many more successes to come.

So yes, you can start over.

You can change your career, you can transfer to another school, you can move to another country. You can even fail the same class three times over the span of ten years like I did and finally pass it on the fourth try.

Understanding your "why" is a strong motivator, and this alongside the resources you will secure on the road to your goal will lead to your accomplishing it. Do not be defeated by a few setbacks; you have it in you to move forward.

MOMENT OF REFLECTION:
"Failure should be our teacher, not our undertaker. Failure is delay, not defeat. It is a temporary detour, not a dead end. Failure is something we can avoid only by saying nothing, doing nothing, and being nothing."
—DENIS WAITLEY

WEEKLY TO-DO:
What is the one thing you've always wanted to do but haven't? If an idea or dream still gets you excited by just thinking

about it, commit to doing one thing this week (i.e., research, writing out a plan, arranging an informational meeting) that will help you move forward. Set a reminder on your calendar to make sure it gets done.

WEEK 2

REMEMBER YOUR WHY

"You have the power within. It's not your past that's going to define who you are, but it's what you believe about yourself, it's what you believe about your own expectations, what is it that you expect from yourself."

—DR. TERERAI TRENT

Imagine writing down your dreams, burying them in the ground like burying a time capsule, then digging them up years later to see you've accomplished all of them. Sounds incredible, huh?

Dr. Tererai Trent did just that—she literally buried a list of her dreams deep into the ground and dug them up years later.

Dr. Trent, scholar, author, humanitarian, educator, among other incredible achievements, tells a story of being born holding a "baton of poverty" handed down through generations. By age eighteen, Dr. Trent was married with four children and without a high school education. When her country, Zimbabwe, gained independence when she was twenty-two years old, American and Australian women entered her village offering resources of empowerment.

One of the American women in town, who was likely in Zimbabwe contributing to post-war recovery and peace-keeping efforts, asked Dr. Trent a question that would change her life: "What are your dreams?"

Dr. Trent and a group of women from the village were asked this question, and Dr. Trent has never forgotten it. After being nudged to speak after everyone else had so, Dr. Trent responded her dream was to receive an undergraduate degree, master's degree, and PhD in America. Her response was ambitious, especially since she did not have a high school diploma.

Customarily, educational achievements were not meant for women in her village. The woman's sole purpose was to raise children. Dr. Trent knew she had dreams inside, but she was conditioned to believe that she was nothing.

As an abused woman, a wife, and a twenty-two year old with four children, Dr. Trent had many people depending on her. But whether or not it was the nudge by the American woman, Dr. Trent was inspired to no longer hold on to the "baton of poverty" that was passed from her ancestors.

Dr. Trent returned home and shared what the American woman had asked her with her mother, who told her to go out and conquer her dreams. Her mother told her, "Write down your dreams and bury them in the same way we bury the umbilical cord."

In Dr. Trent's culture, the umbilical cord is buried when a child is born. This custom occurs because wherever the child eventually travels beyond the village, they will always remember where they come from and be reminded of their self-importance.

After receiving her mother's blessing, it took Dr. Trent twenty years to accomplish what she set out to do. Dr. Trent worked diligently for eight years to earn her high school diploma. Her high school achievement was awarded with a scholarship to study at Oklahoma State University in the United States, where she earned her bachelor's and master's degrees.

Dr. Trent overcame many obstacles over several years while studying in the US—raising her children, enduring an abusive spouse, and trying to make ends meet for her family.

Through it all, Dr. Trent completed her PhD at Western Michigan University and a second master's degree from the University of California, Berkeley.

Today, Dr. Trent has published two children's books, founded a women's empowerment non-profit, and is among Oprah's favorite guests.

Her life's achievements mentioned here are just the tip of the iceberg, and there are even more things to learn from Dr. Trent's story.

Dr. Trent's story should encourage you to remember why you set out on your journey in the first place.

Today may come with its share of lessons, whether they are reminders of the past or reasons to reach for the future. Today is a great day to reflect on what else you must do to accomplish your dreams. Even when Dr. Trent had to retrieve her children's food from trash cans and she considered giving up on school, she reminded herself of why—the "baton of poverty" she was determined to leave behind.

You have the tools at your fingertips to get you back on track. Just don't stop.

MOMENT OF REFLECTION:
"Once we realize we have the power to find that solution within us, we begin to hear the stirring in our own heart, pointing us to something greater than who we are."
—DR. TERERAI TRENT

WEEKLY TO-DO:
Find ten minutes this week to reflect on why you began your journey. Keep asking yourself "Why have I set out to accomplish this?" until you have run out of answers. Sit with your answers and thoughts for a moment. Then, decide what your next step forward should and will be.

WEEK 3

DO YOU MAKE SENSE TO YOU?

"You can only become truly accomplished at something you love. Don't make money your goal. Instead pursue the things you love doing and then do them so well that people can't take their eyes off of you."

—MAYA ANGELOU

Many of the decisions we make are influenced by others. For some, your parents strongly suggested you choose the career with the greatest return on "their" investment. For others, a significant other recommended you on a path that aligned with their path. Or the decision you went with worked out well for someone you admire. Our loved ones' advice and influence is generally well-meaning.

But, if you are truly being honest with yourself, did you *really* choose your current path?

The path you currently are on is perfectly fine, especially if it is working well for you.

While I chose my career in research and data analytics, I'd be remiss not to acknowledge the strong nudge of my mentors. I am good at research and data analysis, as you may also be good at what you currently are doing, but it is still helpful to take the time to reflect on your trajectory whether all is going well or not.

Do you love what you do? Are you progressing forward? Is it what you imagined it would be? Are you ready for change? If you've answered *no* to most of these questions, it's time to consider what *you* believe is the next best step for *you*.

Taraji P. Henson, American actress and producer, talks about being typecast for certain film roles because of the success of her first major lead role in the movie *Baby Boy* in an interview with BET. (BET Networks, 2017)

In her memoir, *Around the Way Girl: A Memoir,* she writes about how she knew she wouldn't move forward in her career as an actress if she didn't stand up for herself and fight against what everyone else thought was best for her.

She wanted to play the "boss lady," so she tried out for strong lead roles such as the movie *Hidden Figures*. Taraji's persistence resulted in her success because she did not only what she was capable of; she did what would be most fulfilling and promising for her. (Henson, 2017)

Just like Taraji, you are capable of doing *exactly* what you want to do!

Taraji's story shows how she was able to fight through such a rigid industry, despite others' concerns *and* the pay disparity if she remained in her typecast roles. You can overcome whatever obstacle is holding you back from your most fulfilling life.

Advocate for yourself like Taraji P. Henson did after her role in *Baby Boy* and make decisions that make sense to *you*! Do what *you* love, and everything else will fall in place. You may become an international superstar!

MOMENT OF REFLECTION:
"You may encounter many defeats, but you must not be defeated. In fact, it may be necessary to encounter the defeats, so you can know who you are, what you can rise from, how you can still come out of it."

—MAYA ANGELOU

WEEKLY TO-DO:
What is the first thought that comes to mind about your path? Write that thought down on a sticky note or a small piece of paper. In three days, revisit the paper with your thought. If it still holds true, commit to one change you will make toward a more fulfilling path.

WEEK 4

EXCUSES DON'T GET RESULTS

———

"Excuses are tools of incompetence used to build bridges to nowhere and monuments of nothingness. Those who use them seldom amount to anything."

—UNKNOWN

I quit dancing within a week of starting high school. I loved dancing, but one day I decided I was done.

I recall telling my mom I enjoyed my afternoon science class more, as dance and science class overlapped, and that was that—dance school was no longer a thing.

I danced in a dance company as a kid for eight years. My years of performing afforded me admission into a dance program in high school—my audition for the program was the most challenging audition-interview I have ever had, even until this day.

Nailing the audition was a proud moment for me because at thirteen years old I was wholeheartedly determined to one day gain admission into Yale University and The Juilliard School to become the dancing doctor.

Have you ever met someone who was extremely excited about doing something, but suddenly changed their trajectory without any explanation?

We all have moments in our lives when we have a drive to accomplish something or to get involved in a cause. We see a chance to participate in a new experience that seems like the opportunity of a lifetime, but at the very last minute we decide to go against our instincts.

If your instincts are urging you to say yes, go with it! Otherwise, your fear of saying yes will become a list of great opportunities missed out on.

What is this pattern of decision-making, you may ask? It's referred to as the "habit of excuses."

Looking back now, I decided not to dance because I felt that I didn't have anything or anyone to dance for anymore. My parents separated and stopped coming to my performances. I was hurt by this, and though my decision at the time seemed valid, this excuse kept me from partaking in an opportunity to pursue my dancing dreams at Juilliard.

Feeling hurt or restless happens, but what explains our sudden repulsion from incredible opportunities like two negative magnets forced to meet?

I assume there must be a force inside of us that continues to pull us away from our best selves.

Our mind is saying, "Not this time, but maybe next time," instead of saying, "Yes! This is the time."

The barrier is not the excuse itself, but it is the fear of the unknown and of falling short that occupies the mind beforehand. In fact, an area of our brain may actually be responsible for our immediate responses to opportunities.

Decision-making takes place in the amygdala, where it associates a stimulus with its emotional value. (Gupta, 2011) The amygdala triggers an autonomic response to the stimulus with emotional value, specifically related to reward and punishment. Though decision-making involves several neural structures and cognitive systems, our brains are conditioned to respond to experiences that we are nervous, afraid, or even excited to participate in. (Gupta, 2011)

I believe we can recondition decision-making responses when we take leaps of faith, which are like diving into the unknown. The benefit of diving in is that you will eventually come out with more experience than you'd ever imagine.

A quote that drives this home is, "The difference between *try* and *triumph* is that '–umph.'" If you don't give yourself that extra *umph* that encourages you to do something that may seem challenging or out of your league, then you will never know what incredible experience lies on the other side of it. At the very least you'd come out with a lesson, and at most something life changing.

When the mind whispers, "Not this time," I challenge you to counter it with, "Now *is* the time because I said that I would do this, so it must be done."

In Denzel Washington's 2017 NAACP speech, he said, "Without commitment, you will never start," and "...more importantly, without *consistency* you'll never finish." (Davis, 2017)

It is not enough to declare that you want the result; each day is a critical step toward reaching your goals. Waiting until tomorrow is not an option because tomorrow is not promised. If we create excuse after excuse for everything that seems scary or impossible, we will never accomplish it.

At thirteen years old I didn't know how creating the excuse not to dance because of my parents would impact my future, but now as an adult I walk boldly into the unknown to reach my goals.

Imagine if you said yes and committed to opportunities and experiences as they presented themselves? Thankfully, every day is a new day to choose you and to recommit to living a life without the burden of excuses. Give yourself permission to get the results that you desire, now!

MOMENT OF REFLECTION:
"You have to grab moments when they happen. I like to improvise and ad lib."
—DENZEL WASHINGTON

WEEKLY TO-DO:

Mel Robbins suggests a method that will help you work around excuses. Starting today, set your alarm for thirty minutes earlier than you typically do, and once it goes off literally throw the covers off, get out of bed, and stand there for ten seconds. This will suck, but once you are up for ten seconds you will stay awake. Challenge yourself to do this and do it with confidence. Use these thirty minutes to work on something you have been intentionally putting off that will propel you toward real and lasting results.

WEEK 5

LET IT GO

"Renew, release, let go. Yesterday's gone. There's nothing you can do to bring it back. You can't "should've" done something. You can only DO something. Renew yourself. Release that attachment. Today is a new day!"

—STEVE MARABOLI

Grudge [gruhj] noun: "a persistent feeling of ill will or resentment resulting from a past insult or injury." (Oxford, 2021)

Defining a commonly used word like "grudge" might seem unnecessary, but it is important to fully understand. Let's focus on three components of a grudge so you can work through it: persistent feeling, ill will or resentment, and past insult or injury.

A persistent feeling occurs over and over again and is a feeling you can't seem to let go of. It's a continuous nudge in your gut or chest that keeps you on edge, resulting from or causing a vivid reminder of what caused the feeling in the first place. The feeling can be anger, fear, excitement, or "butterflies," or it can be a feeling of safety, security, or the opposite of both. Such feelings can remain for days, years, and even a lifetime if they do not dissipate, or we don't find a way to heal from it.

Unfortunately, feelings for many people do not just go away, even if you've worked hard to suppress them. Counseling, meditation, or other support resources can be helpful, as they may offer a renewed sense of control over emotions and a sense of self to recognize when or why certain feelings may be triggered. A change of atmosphere may also be helpful in invoking or healing persistent feelings.

I've struggled with persistent feelings about my responsibilities as a sister-parent, knowing in an "ideal" situation I would only be the sister.

When I agreed to care for my youngest brother indefinitely since he was ten, I knew the road would be tough. I would have to work through my feelings about my mom and his dad's shortcomings. Thankfully, I was able to avoid anger and resentment by going to therapy and expressing my feelings with my closest friends.

The mental and physical manifestation of holding onto resentment, namely in the form of stress, can cause long term health impacts and ill health outcomes. Resentment can lead to the development of misguided behaviors and habits, impacting close relationships with others.

Past injury or insult is a hurtful occurrence that has already happened—key word: past.

Occurrences that happened yesterday can have a bearing on tomorrow, for better or for worse. In the case of holding a grudge, the odds are that the bearing on tomorrow will be worse. This hurtful occurrence is in the past and can't be changed, but we can control how we respond to it. Maybe it matters or it doesn't matter. Maybe it was painful and difficult to overcome, and you have something better now, so it is not worth pondering over. Who knows! What matters here is you have the ability to influence how you will respond to the issue moving forward.

When considering the three components collectively, the definition and *act* of holding a grudge can have larger consequences than probably intended. What is shifting your perspective about the situation, thing, or person worth? Though feelings may be difficult to overcome, letting go frees you of matters that have been occupying your mind and body rent-free.

Give yourself permission to detach, and let the inevitable change attach you to something or someone even better.

MOMENT OF REFLECTION:
"We can't be afraid of change. You may feel very secure in the pond that you are in, but if you never venture out of it, you will never know that there is such a thing as an ocean, a sea. Holding onto something that is good for you now, may be the very reason why you don't have something better."
—C. JOYBELL C.

WEEKLY TO-DO:

What have you had a hard time letting go of? Is it an item, a situation or place, a person? Schedule thirty minutes this week to create a pro and con list of what your life would look like if you finally let it or them go. Then, observe the longer list, and make your decision accordingly.

WEEK 6

THIS, TOO, SHALL PASS

"Just like the moon, we go through phases."
—DULCE RUBY

I suddenly became filled with immense emotion one morning while counting change in my wallet. In the middle of counting, I daydreamed I was counting coins at Whole Foods to purchase a red apple, and because I didn't have enough, I had to return the apple to the shelf. I imagined the other customers in the self-check-out line looking at me, yet no one extended a helping hand.

Unfortunately, I had already excitedly imagined myself slicing the apple in pieces and sprinkling cinnamon on top, then tasting the earthy sweet goodness as it graced my tastebuds, eating it with gratitude.

But it was just that, a vision, one unrealized.

Moments before counting change in my wallet, I wrote myself a check for $10,000,000 with the memo, "Promise to self." I was inspired to do so by an Instagram post that my friend, Rahkim Sabree, author and personal finance enthusiast, posted.

Personal finance has always been a concern of mine. Rahkim's post was motivation to make specific and measurable financial commitments to myself for self-manifestation purposes. I had recently shared with my boss when I would be resigning from my job to prepare for medical school, and the thought of needing enough money to live, support my family, and pay back student loans in the near future was becoming my reality.

I suppose that in the instant of writing the check and then envisioning not having money to buy an apple, the two extremes also became my reality, and the clash electrified me like a negative charge meeting its positive.

At any moment, my lived experience can reflect what I envisioned—not having the money to pay for my basic needs. I admit I have experienced instances in my life when I found just enough coins to pay for food, and I promised myself I would not return to that place ever again. But while there, I reminded myself that my situation was temporary, and I would strategically plan for a financially stable future.

When you have come to terms with a situation you were or currently are in, commit to rewriting your now to reflect the future you imagine. Recycle the energy from both of your extremes, find excitement for what the future will bring, and channel that motivation to keep pressing forward. Your season of abundance is near.

MOMENT OF REFLECTION:

"Yesterday is gone. Tomorrow has not yet come. We have only today. Let us begin."

—MOTHER TERESA

WEEKLY TO-DO:

Do you have a vision of or currently are in a situation that concerns you? Worrying about how to handle the situation can bring anxiety and confusion about how to get past it. Whatever your situation was or is, it is up to you to make sure that it will soon pass. Write down an actionable plan with timelines for how you will no longer allow this situation to occur in your future. If you are unsure how to put your plan into action, ask others' opinions for information and find local or online resources to help you get started.

WEEK 7

THE STRUGGLE MAKES YOU STRONGER

―

"Stop telling yourself you're not qualified, not worthy or not experienced enough. Growth happens when you start doing things you're not qualified to do."

—STEVEN BARTLETT

From a caterpillar to a cocoon, this creature survives the elements—rain, wind, and heat—and evolves into an intricate form. I am very fascinated with the transformation of a butterfly. If you have ever seen a caterpillar, you'd observe how slowly it crawls on the ground or plant and how vulnerable it is to animals and other insects. Imagine the struggle the caterpillar must endure on its way to taking its true form, and to finally fly beyond its chrysalis.

Metamorphosis, defined as "a profound change in form from one stage to the next in the life history of an organism" by dictionary.com, is profound. Changing physical form is a natural occurrence, though I can only imagine how difficult it can be. Human life transformation can be similar.

After catching up with a friend from graduate school while at a conference in 2017, she connected me with her former supervisor in South Africa for a public health research opportunity.

My meeting with her former supervisor led to him offering me the opportunity; though excited and eager to accept, I had no idea how I was going to make it work.

I was working for the government at the time, and I was the sole source of my family's income and insurance. I was paying down credit debt, student loans, my husband was unemployed, and my brother was still adjusting to his new school.

With all of this, something inside of me told me to figure out a way to go to South Africa. After saving just enough money over nine months and receiving some financial support to sustain my family, I mustered the audacity to take a leave of absence from work for about four months to go to South Africa to conduct tuberculosis stigma research.

Working in South Africa was one of the best decisions I've ever made, and one I didn't know would renew my drive toward becoming a doctor. Working in clinics in rural villages showed me the dark side of health care in under-resourced communities much more severe than what I've witnessed at home in the US.

The need for medical supplies, healthcare providers, well-trained staff, and vocal community advocates was immense, and I was hurt by the fact that I was unable to lend my help in a more impactful way beyond the collection of information for research.

In my blog post *Left On The Side of the Road*, I detailed my disdain for how a South African woman, my colleague's sister, was regarded by the healthcare establishment. After witnessing how she was treated, I knew that upon returning home I needed to become the physician my colleague's sister needed that evening in the emergency room. (Young, 2017)

When I returned home that December, the money I saved beforehand and received while working in South Africa was almost gone. We did not have money for Christmas gifts or to travel to Connecticut to be with my immediate family.

To say the struggle was real would be an understatement. We had enough money to cover bills and groceries, and we had each other, *but* my husband and I were determined to conquer our goals and to never struggle in this way again.

Further, while we may be born with abilities, features, and characteristics, we are destined to undergo profound and beautiful transformations just like butterflies, though they may not be changes the world can see. There will inevitably be some mountains to climb before we realize who we really are.

The American Psychological Association explains how we all face trauma, adversity, and other stresses, providing "a roadmap for adapting to life-changing situations, and emerging even stronger than before." (Palmiter et al., 2012)

According to a study by Croft et al., people who have dealt with past adversity reported an increased "capacity for savoring" in the present compared to people currently struggling with adversity who reported "diminished proclivity for savoring positive events." Croft et al. concluded people who have had worse past experiences in life may lead to an eventual upside by promoting the ability to appreciate small pleasures.

Climbing to the mountaintop is parallel to building resilience. In other words, experiencing hardships is inevitable. You will have to throw yourself into opportunities and situations and take paths that might leave you a bit vulnerable.

As frightening and simple as it is, if anyone can get through it, it is you! Just as a diamond is made after carbon is exposed to high pressure and temperature, all you have and will endure will make you well prepared to persevere through other struggles and you will shine brightly!

MOMENT OF REFLECTION:
"Don't feel entitled to anything you didn't sweat and struggle for."

—MARIAN WRIGHT EDELMAN

WEEKLY TO-DO:

What have you struggled to overcome? Take thirty minutes this week to map out one struggle that you are eager to conquer, and list three ways you will get through it and one way you will celebrate afterward.

WEEK 8

OLD WAYS WON'T OPEN NEW DOORS

―――

"The power of intention can open the door of opportunity and transform a valley of trouble into a triumph of joy."
—DEBASISH MRIDHA

My husband tells a story of how he and his college roommate would go out to nightclubs in Washington, DC, return home after 3 a.m., and *then* have to spend the next day from 7 a.m. to 2 a.m. in the architecture lab.

The struggle to remain awake and productive throughout the day was immense, and the pressure to balance fun and the rigor of his program's curriculum was overwhelming.

Have you experienced the struggle of late nights and early mornings? Many of us who attended college remember those long, restless nights. Attempting to wake up after evenings spent partying or hanging out with friends was a nightmare. Just like my husband, I surely wasn't thrilled to start my days, but I had to get up and go to class no matter how I felt.

Waking up after long, fun-filled nights was a testament to your will to succeed. However, relying on your strong knees and gut reactions to start your day will not always save you from trouble or an unproductive day.

Imagine missing an interview because you overslept your alarm. What would you do?

Apologizing for missing the interview may seem like the best option, though every interviewer may not be as forgiving.

Restless evenings followed by tough days can remind us of the importance of refining habits and behaviors that may have worked for us in the past to help secure our future opportunities.

If you have written a paper within an hour or so before it was due, you know exactly what I am talking about. "I write better under pressure" is a common excuse to leave such an important task until the very last minute. This idea leads to channeling superhero-like speed to get the task done, but constantly putting this kind of pressure on yourself can have long-term negative outcomes.

A human being needs oxygen to survive, but too much oxygen can be deadly. It's the same idea with pressure. A little can spur us on to accomplish great things, but too much can crush us like a soda can.

Give yourself time to generate clear thoughts, ask questions, and plan with care.

In the research profession, we plan carefully by creating proposals. According to the University of Southern California's *Research Guides*, there are two reasons for research proposals:

1. to present and *justify* the need to study a research problem
2. to present the *practical* ways in which the proposed study should be conducted.

I use research planning as an example to emphasize this: Do not wait until the last minute to make responsible decisions, as you may just miss your blessing.

What will your old decisions cost you? Think about where you want your life to go. Think of all the ways you have built yourself up, and all the things you built yourself for. Your experiences count toward the next doors that you will open or close.

MOMENT OF REFLECTION:
"When one door closes, another opens; but we often look so long and so regretfully upon the closed door that we do not see the one which has opened for us."
—ALEXANDER GRAHAM BELL

WEEKLY TO-DO:

What new doors do you want to walk through? Do you think they are within reach, or have you made decisions that are pulling you further away from them? Take fifteen minutes this week to consider your proximity to what you desire and make one decision about how you will move a step closer to it.

WEEK 9

WE REPEAT WHAT WE DON'T REPAIR

"You can't go back and change the beginning, but you can start where you are and change the ending."

—C.S. LEWIS

Imagine going years with a broken-down car without getting it repaired. You get the occasional oil and tire changes, yet you never get the electrical, brakes, transmission, and air filters checked. On your way to the grocery store, your car shuts off at a red light.

Thankfully, a kind person uses their jumper cables to restart your car. You drive about ten miles ahead and your car shuts off again.

Another kind person helps with their jumper cables to get you back on the road again. This happens every fifteen miles you drive your car, until one day your car battery dies completely.

Without the funds to purchase a new car, you have a much bigger problem on your hands.

Now, imagine this car is a metaphor for your life. You go on year after year with the same habits and circumstances that are never dealt with. You choose not to confide in professionals to help you through expected and unexpected situations. You've invested time and money into dreams that you gave up on. Your relationships are no longer evolving. You remain in the same state for a long time. There you are, living your life until you suddenly feel unwell.

You visit a professional and you are told the feeling was temporary. Within weeks, you are unwell again. You finally learn your mental, physical, financial, and social health are beyond repair. Unlike a car, you cannot replace your health. If owning a vehicle that has gone years without proper repairs sounds outrageous, the idea of a life without proper support and nurturing should too!

After gaining about thirty pounds over three years due to relationship stress and depression, a visit to my doctor reminded me of why nurturing my health is important. She told me I was pre-diabetic and I had small fibroids, and the latter could lead to infertility if they grow and are not surgically removed in time.

My doctor told me I could turn my diagnoses around by leading a healthier lifestyle, which included eating more fruits and vegetables, less fast food, and regular exercise.

I took her advice and made drastic changes—I stopped eating red meat and hired a personal trainer to jumpstart my fitness efforts. I also let go of my toxic relationship and vowed to not enter another one like it again. Not only did I attain the best physical and mental health of my life, but I also made an intentional effort to repair something properly the first time that could have been impossible to reverse.

Like our physical health, our personal wellness is impacted when we choose other things, people, or circumstances over ourselves, though it's not to say we should ignore our responsibilities. It means we need to perform regular self-checks on our personal health. Our bodies, minds, and interactions are not material possessions that can be recycled and have unlimited numbers of repairs.

It is helpful to have assistance from loved ones and professionals to keep us on track to a healthier well-being. We continue to choose what's most convenient, cheap, or easiest at our own expense, repeating this potentially detrimental cycle.

Commit to repairing aspects of yourself that will contribute to a best possible life. Do not risk running out of time because you waited until the very last minute.

MOMENT OF REFLECTION:
"We all make mistakes, have struggles, and even regret things in our past. But you are not your mistakes, you are here now with the power to shape your day and your future."

—STEVE MARABOLI

WEEKLY TO-DO:

Today is a great day to get something done you have been putting off for too long. Make the call. Schedule the appointment. Make the change. Do it today! So you don't forget, write it on a sticky note, schedule it in your phone, or set an alarm.

WEEK 10

LISTEN TO YOUR DREAM

―――

"Hope lies in dreams, in imagination, and in the courage of those who dare to make dreams into reality."
—JONAS SALK

I was confident I would attend a good university because of my competitive academic profile and extensive community service, but I was not exactly sure where. Early in the application season I received several acceptances, but I did not feel a particular connection with the universities.

One morning, I awoke to a very vivid replay of a dream of me speaking to Dr. Martin Luther King, Jr. This sounds ridiculous and a bit cliché, but I had a dream that Dr. King told me to go to Washington, DC for college and shared an empowering message about taking risks for a successful future.

I thought it all very strange indeed, particularly because this was the first dream that I remembered, but I said to myself, "Alright then," and I embraced it.

I shared my dream with my oldest brother that morning.

He casually said, "Okay, then go to DC."

I took his "go to DC" as my confirmation to lean into the prospect of attending college there.

The very thought of Dr. King's legacy in the United States and world history as a civil rights leader was and is enough to convince me that my dream was prophetic. My fervor toward the healing of and advocating for Black communities in America as a girl mirrored the voice of Dr. King in his relentless fight for justice and civil rights for all.

My eagerness is the primary reason I wanted to attend college in the first place. When the decision came to choose between one of the two universities in DC I applied to and was accepted into, I committed to attending Georgetown University because of its guiding principles, zeal for service, and the support it would offer me on my academic and professional journeys.

Four years later in my final year of college, I was the Innovation Speaker at the Dr. Martin Luther King, Jr. Let Freedom Ring Concert at the John F. Kennedy Center for the Performing Arts.

The invitation to speak reminded me of my dream as if it was déjà vu. What fascinated and scared me the most was that I was commemorating Dr. King and addressing President Barack Obama at the same time. I also met Dr. King's speechwriter, Mr. Clarence Jones, an introduction that truly felt like I had prophetically come full circle with my own speech that evening.

My obvious nervousness before the address and photo with the Obamas caught the eye of the late legendary John Thompson, Jr., former NBA player and championship-winning Georgetown Men's Basketball coach.

Coach Thompson gently sat down next to me and said, "One day you will be in a room with kings and queens. Just know you belong there." His words calmed me, and I felt an overwhelming sense of confidence and belonging overcome me.

I leaned into my dream, unaware of where it would take me.

At seventeen years old, I left home for college to experience the unknown and unexpected, to come full circle as if the path were already laid out for me.

You, too, are destined to discover incredible experiences if you allow yourself to trust the vision of your dreams.

I did not know anyone who had taken such a leap of faith as I had done when I moved to DC for college. I also had no clue what the outcomes would be, but confidence, prayer, hard work, persistence, and perseverance were my parachutes.

Every opportunity that comes your way will feel uncertain and seemingly strange at times, yet their promise requires you to boldly and confidently lean into them.

According to ABC's *Hidden Truths' Are in Those Dreams*, commuters in a study revealed, "Some 68 percent said that dreams foretell the future, and 63 percent said at least one of their dreams had come true." (Dye, 2009)

At such a high probability, the likelihood of your dreams telling you something and of you accomplishing your goals should be enough to convince you to lean into them. If this statistic isn't enough, let my journey be a firm example that dreams are real and they, in fact, come true with effort.

MOMENT OF REFLECTION:
"The only limit to the height of your achievements is the reach of your dreams and the willingness to work hard for them."
—MICHELLE OBAMA

WEEKLY TO-DO:
Have you had a dream or an inkling lately that you felt was encouraging you to do something bold and outrageous? Do you think there are benefits of leaning into this dream? Take twenty minutes this week, while lying in bed or working out, to imagine what life would be like if you say yes.

WEEK 11

COMMIT ON PURPOSE

―

"You always have two choices: your commitment versus your fear."

—SAMMY DAVIS, JR.

We can create an excuse for just about anything. We make excuses for things we know must get done and leave them to the last minute, as well as for things we don't want to do instead of just saying no outright.

Many excuses we make are much bigger and sometimes get in the way of our goals whether we realize it or not. Your plans may conflict with your current comforts. The person who may have been interested in investing in your brilliant start-up idea may have been at the party you RSVP'd yes to, but the couch was too cozy. Oops!

Your word can create a tug-of-war between comfort and commitment. If you told someone or yourself that you will get something done, it's typically best to err on the side of your word unless it is an emergency or critical change of direction.

When I tell someone I am going to do something, I do it, even if when the day arrives I no longer want to. If I tell Tawana, my sister and best friend, that I'm going shopping with her after a long commute to Connecticut from DC, I'm going shopping because I said I would and I love her. I pride myself in being a person of my word, and this alone has created unexpectedly good opportunities.

The only caveat to not doing what I said I would is if I am completely mentally and physically exhausted *and* I communicated in advance that I can no longer do what I was asked.

I recognize if I am serious about my accomplishing goals and upholding my character, I must prioritize my commitments regardless of how small.

It is also extremely important to *understand when to say no* to commitments to prioritize your own health. If you are unsure of how to say no, reach out to a mentor, trusted loved one, or a professional to learn strategies about how to do so.

Let's also consider how to stick to your commitments. It starts with a plan.

The moment you commit to doing something, write it down and use your calendar. Either make a mental note of how close or far out the commitment is or include a reminder in your schedule about it (for example, create an alert ion your device for three to seven days in advance). You can do this for commitments that you have made to others and commitments you have made to *yourself*.

The plan you develop for yourself should be made plain—be very specific about what you want by writing it down, drawing a picture, or printing a large image. This may seem a bit dramatic, but it's effective! Use tools such as a computer or phone background to visualize it, whether it's on the lock screen or main screen.

In addition to visualization, your plan needs to have a realistic timeline.

Now, how can you navigate the time you have right now to fit in progress toward the goal, perhaps five minutes a day or three times a week? Further, how do you use the time productively so you can *actually* make progress?

Make a list of one to three tasks that you will complete that day or during your chosen timeframe. Also, let someone close to you know about your commitment so they can keep asking you about it (annoying, but effective!).

Jackson et al. conducted a study that found if you have a specific accountability appointment with someone who you made the commitment to or with, you will increase your chance of success by up to 95 percent. (Jackson, 2015)

Don't let your pride get in the way of your commitment and remember to ask for help if you need it. Help from others makes the dream happen!

Even if you think help is not within reach, take a moment to figure out where you can get it from. If it's not from friends or family, how about an online workshop, a conference, or a networking opportunity?

Ever considered cold calling, emailing, or DM-ing ("direct messaging") someone who can assist you? I did all the above for this book's pre-order campaign, and it was successful!

Making a commitment to yourself requires figuring out the impossible to make it possible. Push all excuses aside and start making moves. Pride and fear can be dream-deniers. Let's make a declaration: "I will follow through on my commitment by any and all means necessary."

MOMENT OF REFLECTION:
"Commitment leads to action. Action brings your dream closer."
—MARICA WIEDER

WEEKLY TO-DO:
Be creative with your commitment. In addition to scheduling and visualizing your commitments, take one hour this week to research new tools, opportunities, and people who can help you with your goal. Once you have found one, even if you are unsure it will be exactly what you need, be bold and reach out by email, phone, or DM.

WEEK 12

THE HUSTLE IS SOLD SEPARATELY

"No one gets very far unless he accomplishes the impossible at least once a day."

—ELBERT HUBBARD

Whether you were born into wealth and can use your influence to accomplish your dreams, or you were born into poverty and have to get creative, getting the chance to live out your dream is what matters.

The hustle to get there is a different story. And for many, the journey toward your goals can feel impossible.

As humans, we tend to automatically think about the hurdles instead of the triumphs. The person you have to become on your journey is different from the person you were when you dreamt it.

When you envision yourself in the future your imagination illustrates a world of opportunities. Your mindset will shift when you believe you can and will achieve these opportunities. To get beyond your imagination to realize your dream, making some sacrifices will be important.

Ask yourself, *Am I willing to be uncomfortable? Am I willing to endure delayed gratification? Can I withstand judgement? If I am misunderstood by friends and family, will I continue reaching forward? Am I willing to do absolutely what it takes to succeed?*

A survivor of sex-trafficking, Shay found answers to these questions and refuge in education.

In our conversation, Shay shared she could only imagine what freedom to live life as *she* wanted would be like since she was in grade school.

As a victim of sex-trafficking as a pre-teen, there was no safe way out of her situation for over a decade. Shay was unaware of resources within reach that could help her, but eventually she confided in a trusted person because she was committed to a safe and successful future.

Because Shay had *permission* from her victimizer to remain in school but not going far for college, she leveraged the school's resources such as becoming involved in activities, clubs, and doing well academically to incrementally get further and further away from her life outside of school.

Shay survived, acknowledging many women who were trafficked with her did not, and now is a fantastic mother and is working in her dream career. Shay did what she must for as long as it needed to take to live a free and purpose-driven life.

Your experiences and trajectory may be different than Shay's but having the will to make your own decisions should be enough to propel you farther in life than where you are now.

Dreaming about what your life can be is the first step but hustling to make your dreams come through is another.

Grinding is not hustling. *Grinding* is constantly putting in *hard work* to find the next move for your dream and *hustling* is making *efficient and strategic* moves to get closer to the dream. Hard work is certainly required but having a strategic mindset while working is critical.

The point is to start. You have to pave your own way forward, even if the odds are against you.

Shay found her way forward by centering education and working diligently to escape her lived situation, though it was not easy. If Shay can do it, you can do it. The hustle is yours!

MOMENT OF REFLECTION:
"Hard work beats talent if talent doesn't work hard."
—TIM NOTKE, BASKETBALL COACH

WEEKLY TO-DO:

Take thirty minutes this week to think about a dream that you have been working very hard toward, but you don't seem to be making progress on. Consider the steps you have been taking. Are you close to or far away from accomplishing your goal? Write down two possible strategies for you to get to your goal. Choose the strategy most specific and efficient. Start executing!

WEEK 13

A PASS FORWARD

"Life can only be understood backwards; but it must be lived forwards."

—SØREN KIERKEGAARD

How can you plan for the future if you never processed your past?

Our past gives us insight into experiences we have lived through, the choices we've made, and why we've decided to make our journeys in the first place. It also contextualizes our present experiences and choices, providing explanations that may not be obvious without reflection.

It is good to know that the work required to dive into the past can be helpful and our futures, as a result, can be crafted with intention. Our futures do not exist in a vacuum. How we deal with the future is based on all our past experiences and learned tools. Your past is much more than small pieces of a bigger picture or blemishes to be forgotten; these pieces are *keys* to the future you desire.

I had a traumatic encounter with a supervisor in one of my first professional jobs, and I buried it in my mind because I was afraid that it would happen to me again. While I have been able to navigate my career without experiencing the encounter again, it was difficult for me to trust anyone I worked with following the incident.

I recalled the situation in therapy about ten years later, and I had a breakthrough. It wasn't trust alone I was grappling with; additionally, I did not want to be hurt again by someone I looked up to.

After coming to this understanding, my relationship with supervisors or managers have been more collaborative, and it also helped me develop better management skills and to trust others.

Like me, you may be reminded of situations you had to dig yourself out of and promised yourself you'd never revisit that place again too. Reflecting on your past may even unveil deep-rooted traumas that affect you. Such traumas have a hold on your progress, preventing you from fully achieving the life you imagine.

Therapy with a psychologist helped me immensely; for some, speaking to the person or dealing with the matter firsthand helped them. Whatever you choose to do, develop a strategy around these three questions:

1. How have I been affected by this experience?
2. What will it take for me to heal from this experience and move forward?

3. What do I hope to gain from talking about and working through this experience?

Choose not to carry past feelings of regret, anger, and fear into your future. Experiences you may have inherited or developed are not permanent declarations on your life; you can let them go. Your past may have influenced the path you have taken so far but should not define your path forward. Your future is one thing you have control over if you give yourself permission to let go of what was and embrace what can be. The experiences you embrace should be infused with love, trust, and pure joy.

While you do not have to right every wrong of your past, acknowledge the parts that have taken hold of you for so long. Do whatever it takes to work through it, and then give yourself a pass to live freely, boldly, and confidently forward.

MOMENT OF REFLECTION:
"It doesn't matter who you are, where you come from. The ability to triumph begins with you. Always." —Oprah Winfrey

WEEKLY TO-DO:
When was the last time you gave yourself permission to be free to do as you please mentally, physically, and emotionally? Take one hour this week to free yourself from anything that was causing you distress in the moment, in the past, or what is to be in the future. Dance, sing, read, or do whatever gives you the feeling of joy and freedom to be unapologetically yourself.

WEEK 14

PAY YOURSELF FIRST

―――

"Rest is a wealth strategy."
—MARSHAWN EVANS DANIELS

"Secure your own mask first before assisting others." We take this advice seriously while in flight, but if we were to apply this line practically to our daily lives, we'll more than likely realize we typically put others before ourselves.

Helping others is honorable, but too often we go above and beyond for others before we assess our own needs. We forget that maintaining our mental and emotional health gives us the ability to be present for others, whether that's showing up for a stranger, siblings, or our children. Mindfulness of our actions helps to keep our lives as balanced as possible, steering clear of putting ourselves at risk.

My financial adviser told me and my husband to save 25 percent for three months of living expenses in the case of an emergency. We have yet to save three months' worth of living expenses, but the idea of paying ourselves into an account for immediate needs, like a tire repair or family emergency, stays at the front of my mind.

"In case of an emergency" can seem far-fetched, but there is no point in trying to predict a situation when you can just be prepared for it.

In the words of Suga Free, "If you stay ready you don't have to get ready."

Growing up in a low-income family, we never had extra money. If a crisis happened, like the loss of our occasional car or social services (i.e., food vouchers, health insurance, bill payment assistance, etc.), we didn't have many resources or a reliable support network to call on. Anything beyond food, shelter and water felt out of reach, including our mental wellness because of these concerns.

I mention my past life in hopes that you're reminded of a time in your life when a set of circumstances made it difficult to achieve stability and caused important things to be put on the back burner. You have the opportunity to change that today!

Be mindful of the resources you have access to and recognize that every support you rely on may not be available forever, be it your job or your babysitter. Put things in place for yourself now so that you have a better handle on shortcomings when they arise.

Self-care is self-payment; you are rewarding yourself with things that will ensure your short- and long-term well-being.

Invest in your health, your sanity, your bank account, and your ideas, and make sure you are happy with your personal investments before deciding if you can afford to invest your resources in others.

When you have more, you'll have some to share, and those who you help will benefit from your generosity with sincerity.

MOMENT OF REFLECTION:
"Do not save what is left after spending but spend what is left after saving."
—WARREN BUFFET

WEEKLY TO-DO:
Do this every day this week: in the morning when you wake, eat a good meal and workout before you feed the dog and take it for a walk—this is not selfish; this is self-care. Before you head out to work or class in the morning, have a quick self-check in (try talking to yourself in the mirror) to make sure you are in a good state to tackle the day—this is not an excuse to not go; this is self-care. When you receive some form of reward this week, whether your paycheck or as a gift, set aside a percentage of it (for example, 2 percent, 5 percent, 50 percent)—this isn't being frugal; this is self-care. When you have accomplished something major this week and your friends want to celebrate but you'd rather rest, don't go—this isn't being ungrateful; this is self-care. Choose YOU first this week.

WEEK 15

YES TO NEW FRIENDS

"Each friend represents a world in us, a world possibly not born until they arrive, and it is only by this meeting that a new world is born."

—ANAIS NIN

There's nothing like a really good person who catches your vibe, and you also catch their vibe instantly. Whether you're shopping at the grocery store, at a bar, or just walking in a park, you might connect with someone over a really short, unpredictable conversation. You might even want to spend more time with them to get to know each other a little better—not in a romantic way, per se, but in a friendly way.

For many who have adopted the "I don't need new friends" persona, I want to make a declaration: *There is nothing wrong with making new friends!*

This notion of refusing to make new friends because your current or "day ones" are great doesn't mean you don't have room for new ones.

We grow as we get older, when we travel the world, and when we encounter and interact with different environments, each of which can benefit from having friends with varied viewpoints and experiences. Welcoming new people into your life can introduce you to perspectives and activities your current friends may not know about or have access to.

I ran into a colleague from graduate school at a public health conference who I hadn't seen since graduation. In graduate school, we shared a friend group and a few classes together. We stayed in touch post-graduation on Facebook infrequently, so I was aware she had been working in international public health for a few years.

When we ran into each other, we caught up on our whereabouts and professional ventures since we last saw each other, emphasizing her work in West Africa during the 2014–2016 Ebola outbreak.

So amazed by the work she had done, I made an off-the-cuff comment that ended up changing my life: "I am sure I am the only one in our cohort who has never worked abroad."

My colleague asked me if I wanted to work abroad in a public health capacity, and I casually responded, "Of course." She immediately asked if it was okay to refer me to her former supervisor in South Africa whose organization may be interested in a short-term researcher.

I agreed, sent her my résumé, and within days I spoke to her former supervisor on Skype, who then invited me to South Africa to contribute to their tuberculosis and HIV research.

I accepted the offer, taking a leave of absence from my government job, and my time there was the best few months of my life, personally and professionally.

This is all to say that the new people we meet have no context for our past and no information about our future, and because of this, they are open to getting to know the *present* you. Many are eager to know your interests and willing to connect you to opportunities you didn't know existed. The *present* you requires people and opportunities with fresh and unbiased perspectives that will fulfill your needs now.

Whether the new people you meet are meant to be in your life for a short season or to become your new best friend, you should remain in touch by sharing phone numbers or social media handles. You never know where that relationship might take you.

In some cases, new friends may have more to offer your journey right now than your current friends. Your current friends can be engaging and supportive too, but there is room to invite others to elevate you toward the future you desire.

I'd be remiss not to mention that in some cases, letting go of old friends may not be so bad either. The Mayo Clinic suggests that maintaining old friendships may be difficult due to having grown apart as you grow and your interests change.

> *"Many adults find it hard to develop new friendships or keep up existing friendships. Friendships may take a back seat to other priorities, such as work or caring for children or aging parents. You and your friends*

may have grown apart due to changes in your lives or interests. Or maybe you've moved to a new community and haven't yet found a way to meet people." (Mayo Clinic, 2019)

If you are having trouble finding new friends, the Mayo Clinic also suggests attending community events, volunteering, extending and accepting invitations, taking up a new interest, joining a faith community, or simply taking a walk.

The next time you find yourself vibing with someone new, invite them into the spaces most comfortable for you and see how it goes. You have everything to gain from new friendships, even if it's a lesson.

MOMENT OF REFLECTION:
"Right now, someone you haven't met is out there wondering what it would be like to meet someone like you."
—UNKNOWN

WEEKLY TO-DO:
When was the last time you met someone new or followed up with someone who you recently met? Take five minutes this week to reach out to a new friend or colleague by email, DM, or text, and ask if they would like to chat over coffee or lunch.

WEEK 16

DOING WHAT'S MOST DIFFICULT

―

"The hardest part of any important task is getting started on it in the first place. Once you actually begin work on a valuable task, you seem to be naturally motivated to continue."

—BRIAN TRACY

Ever wake up in the morning and just lay there, not wanting to get up because it's so warm and comfortable? Good sleep makes you want to drift back into it as though there are no pressing matters to attend to, yet you have so much to do. Despite your comfort, you push yourself to get up, which can be one of the most difficult tasks to start your day with.

Whether your morning includes a fitness routine, completing an assignment, or meal preparation, as dreadful as they may seem, these are accomplishments that must get done immediately.

According to the *Productive Engineer*, "Research shows that people who execute their most difficult tasks first are generally more productive and high-achieving than those who start easy and work their way up." (Jimmy 2021) People are also more likely to *complete* the hardest task when done first. For you high achievers, this sounds like a good challenge, right?

It is always a good feeling to know that you have already completed your hardest task, especially when done in the morning. For me, fitness first thing in the morning is my daily struggle. Maintaining a healthy weight is difficult due to my sedentary lifestyle, but I am inspired to wake up early to move to prevent health issues in the future. Though there have been many mornings when I've chosen sleep over fitness, when I actually get up and work out, I feel incredible afterward.

I recognize I will not always get it right, despite my own advice in this chapter. Working out will continue to be difficult if I let it be. But the days I do get it right, I am thrilled and tired, but mostly thrilled.

Have you ever completed a difficult task and afterward you were glad it was done and over with? I feel a surge of energy once I finally dance it out for an hour, and it feels great! The reality with getting any task done is there will always be something else we'd rather be doing or some other tasks that will get in the way.

Fighting the "I'll just do it tomorrow" trap will take some level of stick-to-it-iveness.

In NPR's *Hidden Brain* podcast episode "Creatures of Habit," Dr. Wendy Wood talks about how much of the things we do every day are done without thinking, emphasizing how repeated behavior eventually becomes automatic. She shares her story about wanting to develop the habit of running in the morning before her day with her children and work begins. With her busy life getting the best of her, she tried to figure out ways to make it easier for her to run as planned. One of her plans eventually worked—she wore her running clothes to bed and kept her running shoes nearby. She did this to give herself no excuse not to run when her alarm went off. (Vedantam et al., 2019)

Dr. Wood met herself 90 percent of the way, and by doing so, what was once a difficult task became much easier. She checked off something tough and important first thing in the morning, giving herself the flexibility and time to help her children and get other things done throughout the day. (Vedantam et al., 2019)

Whatever you must get done, try to get the difficult things done first and start making this practice a habit. And, once you have completed them, reward yourself and find the joy in the accomplishment!

MOMENT OF REFLECTION:
"Do the hard jobs first. The easy jobs will take care of themselves."
—DALE CARNEGIE

WEEKLY TO-DO:

Think of a difficult task that needs to be completed in the short term. Consider the reasons why you have yet to get it done. Take thirty minutes this week to figure out ways to make it easier for you to get tasks done. Apply the method that works to other things you've been putting off.

WEEK 17

WHO SAID YOU COULDN'T?

"If I can't work with you, I will work around you."
—ANNIE EASLEY

"You can't do it." The easiest way to get me to do something hard and challenging, whether I want to do it or not, is to tell me I can't.

It's not a matter of whether I can or cannot do it, it's a matter of willingness. *Am I willing to put in the work? Am I willing to go the extra mile? Am I willing to do what everybody else is doing instead of doing it in my own way?* To truly rile me is to tell me, *"You cannot do this."*

When I was a sophomore in college, I planned my course schedule to prepare me to apply to medical school. Having gone to one of the most competitive universities in the United States, the premedical students were extremely competitive, and the science courses were difficult.

I excelled in the humanities and social sciences but adjusting to the natural sciences was difficult. Declared as a biology major, it was beginning to look like spending countless hours in the lab and the library was not the best fit for me.

I scheduled a meeting with my dean in hopes he could recommend a new academic plan so I could complete my pre-med requirements. Having looked at my transcript, my dean said, "You might as well choose a different major or a different route because you're not going to become a doctor."

This dean *declared* I was not going to become a doctor. So instead of providing an academic roadmap to meet my needs and medical aspirations—for example, post-baccalaureate programs, completing summer courses, or revising my schedule to manage one natural science course at a time— this dean outright *told* me I would not become a doctor.

The audacity!

In that moment I felt destroyed, as I could not fathom the idea that my dream was no longer available to me. Not formally being classified as "premed" or being a biology major was one thing, but for someone to declare what my life would be based on the few courses I had already taken toward my degree was another.

The final straw was imagining how many other students he had discouraged from following their dreams.

I chose to never visit that dean again for academic advice. I channeled the hurt into action, and I committed to making sure that students who come from backgrounds underrepresented in medicine knew that they could become doctors with the support of their student peers and by strategically using resources that were made available at the university.

I worked diligently, not just for other students, but for myself. I figured out how being a student leader could gain me access to financial and professional resources that I could make available to everyone else seeking a very similar journey.

With this, I noticed that the students without access to resources were predominately Black, Latinx, and first-generation college students. In fact, the lack of diverse and underrepresented students completing pre-medical coursework at my college reflected the current climate of medicine across the United States. Research highlights the need for an intervention to increase racial and ethnic diversity among medical students, medical school faculty, and the physician workforce. (Price et al., 2009; Khullar, 2018; Lett et al., 2019) If Black, Latinx, and first-generation students had inadequate resources and support during their pre-medical years, the medical workforce would continue to lack diversity.

Through researching, networking, and advocating for our needs, I learned about different avenues to becoming a doctor. I learned that I didn't need to be a natural science major to apply to medical school. The information I gathered at conferences, internship and shadowing opportunities, and course planning advice from medical students I shared with other premed students.

My path would look very different from other premed students' paths, and while I knew I might take a little longer than expected (though not as long as it eventually did), I was comforted in knowing my drive to help other students who may be subjected to the same disappointing advice as I had received would soon pay off.

I am very proud to say, over a decade later, it did pay off.

Channeling hurtful declarations over your life into something positive and greater than yourself is not always easy, but it is certainly not the responsibility of anyone else to tell you how to live your life as you desire it to be. You can do whatever you want to do with your life; sometimes you just have to find the road less travelled to get there. Anyone who puts you down or doubts your ability to achieve something you are really excited about are either jealous of you, they have something against you (of which can be implicit or explicit biases), or they truly do not want you to succeed.

Be aware of what people have to say about your dreams. Choose your journey because you genuinely want to. Nevertheless, if the fire in you still burns, pursue your dreams relentlessly and show the world that your dreams can and will be accomplished.

MOMENT OF REFLECTION:

"The important thing is to realize that no matter what people's opinions may be, they're only just that—people's opinions. You have to believe in your heart what you know to be true about yourself. And let that be that."

—MARY J. BLIGE

WEEKLY TO-DO:

Sometimes we really want to do certain things, but the opinion(s) of people around us prevent us from moving forward. Be mindful of people's opinions of your desires this week. If you are really excited about trying something out or pursuing a particular direction, consult your trusted friends, mentors, or loved ones and get their help in mapping out the road to get you there.

WEEK 18

CONNECT WITH YOURSELF

"Who looks outside, dreams; who looks inside, awakes."
—CARL GUSTAV JUNG

What is the purpose of life? While we won't dive into Nietzsche or Aristotle lessons, there is something innately intriguing about the answers we seek.

We feel that purpose exists because we have interests and desires to be "something" for ourselves and for others. We grow with age, revealing a new set of interests, goals, and wants that can shift what we thought was our purpose. As adults, when we try to find that purpose, it can seem so much harder to grab hold of than we once thought.

We might even think of others as lucky, who have been on the same journey from day one and seem to know exactly why they exist. While other people's experiences appear to be out of reach, such manifestations of "living" may distract you from connecting with your own purpose.

People of faith take on "soul work" to discover their purpose, whether it involves connecting with a higher power or through meditative practice. Many leaders and philanthropists dive into service to discover their purpose, finding meaning in doing good for others.

For me, I leaned into my curiosities about the health of the poor. It took working in another country for a lightbulb to turn on that finally gave meaning to my interest and pulled on my heart in ways I've never felt. The clarity I had is difficult to articulate. I no longer just knew my *what*; I completely understood my *why*.

I rediscovered my zeal to serve as a medical professional to advocate for and give a voice to disenfranchised, overlooked, and underserved populations who live with preventable health conditions and suffer from disparate health outcomes.

I saw my family in the eyes of mothers, aunts, and brothers who desperately sought healthcare to live long enough to see their children grow and to celebrate milestones.

I am not encouraging you to do something out of the ordinary to discover your purpose. However, I personally found that living in an unfamiliar place left me to my own devices because I had no family or known resources to always rely on.

I simply experienced life strategically yet without reservation. After months of navigating all things foreign, talking myself through experiences, praying for strength when I missed home, and immersing myself into my interests (public health and clinical care), I finally saw the light at the end of the tunnel.

While you can probably identify physical things that you care for, what pulls at your soul? Have you experienced the spark that gives you a reason to *truly* live? If you have yet to think deeply about this, I encourage you to find a practice or a place that motivates you to connect with yourself.

Ask yourself: *Who am I? What do I represent? Why do I like the things I like? Why do I converse with certain people? Why do I work where I work?*

These questions may sound ridiculous, but when you are on a journey to claim your worth and to figure out what your reason is for living, for thriving, and for sharing yourself with the world, it is necessary to think intentionally about yourself.

Also, while you are on your journey to connect with yourself, give yourself grace.

MOMENT OF REFLECTION:
"People are like stained-glass windows. They sparkle and shine when the sun is out, but when the darkness sets in their true beauty is revealed only if there is light from within."
—ELISABETH KÜBLER-ROSS

WEEKLY TO-DO:

Close your eyes and imagine the life you want. What do you see? How does it feel? Write down this vision and reflect on why you *really* desire this life and how living this life will help you reveal your purpose.

WEEK 19

DON'T LET THE INTERNET RUSH YOU

"Mostly, the world sees you the way you see yourself."
—LISA NICHOLS

I prepared for my sixth annual professional headshot photo like I was auditioning for a beauty pageant—face beat to the gods, stylish hairdo, vibrant dress, and a twinkle in my eyes to draw in my audience.

My colleagues, friends, and family had to see me for the professional I was, even though I had yet to secure my white coat.

Every year I was not a doctor pressured me to *show* I was still growing in my career.

What better way to illustrate my growth than through a poised and flawless photo and an up-to-date LinkedIn profile?

I admit, I absolutely love taking pictures, but taking professional headshots every year is a bit much. I fell into the mindset that my life had to appear perfect, regardless if I was a doctor or not.

It sure did not help to scroll my social media timelines to see updates from seemingly everyone about landing dream jobs, paired with dreamy vacations, lavish weddings, and perfect babies.

Meanwhile, I was struggling to pass one class for the *fourth* time, paying down debt, and arguing with my pre-teen brother to turn off WWE and go to bed!

Of course, we want to post similar experiences to those we see on social media! Nothing is wrong with wanting and appearing to have everything you've ever wanted out of life. But too often, we become entrenched in what others have and then we impatiently rush to grab ahold of what we think we want.

That's some serious FOMO, fear of missing out.

Glennon Doyle, author of the *New York Times* nonfiction best-seller *Untamed*, said it best in her interview with Marie Forleo:

"*What scares me more than feeling it all is missing it all…the impact of capitalism which tells us all the things we need to be happy and to fit in.*" As someone who seemed to have the perfect life, as a mom and wife to her husband at the time, she too struggled to live with integrity and to be the person who she knew she was within.

Seeking to fit into other people's worlds causes us to lose sight of our own personal journeys and commitments, making us think that just because someone else has something right now, we should have it right now too. The reality is we don't always need everything we see or hear about to lead honest and fulfilling lives.

And quite frankly, I really didn't need to take a fancy photo every year to prove that I was evolving because I surely didn't owe anyone an explanation.

Doyle also mentions in her interview, "The difference between what you see and what you have may be action." (MarieTV, 2020) While rushing to do everything isn't ideal, it is still important to take an unashamed step forward for your own sake. This is not a move to prove to everyone else that you can do it; it is for *you*.

Give yourself permission to enjoy your life as it is and appreciate where you are today. You'd be surprised at how fabulous your life is already and on its way to becoming. You have nothing to prove to anyone.

MOMENT OF REFLECTION:
"Unreasonable haste is the direct road to error."

—MOLIERE

WEEKLY TO-DO:

Take ten minutes this week to reflect on what you want for your life right now. It will be tempting to consider what the future will hold but try to resist planning too far ahead—consider your life one year from now. Whichever "want" keeps coming to mind, write down three steps you will take to make it happen. Try to refrain from scrolling social media while completing this exercise.

WEEK 20

RECLAIM YOUR TIME

"You will never find time for anything. If you want time, you must make it."

—CHARLES BUXTON

I often find myself trying to figure out how to get *everything* done, rather than narrowing in on what actually needs to get done *today*. The anxiety of whether I am doing enough, prioritizing the right things, or finishing what I've started torments me.

My mentor, a respected physician, former government official, and medical school dean, said to me, "You are *always* busy."

I've heard this many times before, but when she said it, I felt an instant sadness. I thought, *What am I doing that keeps me so "busy?"* What does "busy" even mean? What saddened me the most was how she said it—so matter of fact, even though I thought she understood that family, work, and community service responsibilities in my daily life kept me "busy."

I defended myself—bills must be paid, bellies must be fed, and heads must remain covered. In other words, my busyness allows me and my family to live comfortably.

Afterward, I rushed off to my next meeting, but this time with a burning urge to do something different about this so-called "busyness." I recalled reading an article about the benefits of a walking meeting, which is "a meeting that takes place during a walk instead of in an office, boardroom, or coffee shop where meetings are commonly held." (Clayton et al., 2015) So, I decided to combine my meeting and my daily walk, doing both at the same time.

This did not solve my "busy" problem at all; but, helped me to kill two birds with one stone. I strategically doubled down so I could free up an hour.

Staying busy isn't a bad thing if what you are doing is manageable. In fact, research has found that staying busy improves brain function, especially as we get older. (Festini et al., 2016)

"Having a busy schedule was associated with better brain processing, improved memory, sharper reasoning and better vocabulary," according to a *Frontiers in Aging Neuroscience* study. The key is to find a balance between maintaining a healthy schedule and making time for the things and people you love.

Being told "You are *always* busy" resulted in my having something to prove, not only to my loved ones but to myself. I probably needed to revisit my calendar and scratch off a few meetings, tasks, and activities so I could have more time for myself and my family.

While I recognize that the probability of totally freeing up my schedule is nearly impossible, at the very least I have a newfound *intentionality* about how I use my time, and it is at the forefront of my mind. It's my hope for all of us that our anxiety about getting everything done will become calmer and more focused.

MOMENT OF REFLECTION:
"I recommend you take care of the minutes, and the hours will take care of themselves."
—EARL OF CHESTERFIELD

WEEKLY TO-DO:
Pair two tasks or activities in your day that won't conflict if done together. Did you gain an hour? Did your priorities shift? Did you create more "me" time? Make ten minutes this week to reflect on how pairing such tasks or activities made you feel and if you will try it again.

WEEK 21

BREATHE IN, BREATHE OUT

"Between stimulus and response there is a space. In that space is our power to choose our response. In our response lies our growth and our freedom."

—VIKTOR E. FRANKL

Sigh. There's always something getting in the way of your peace of mind. Morning traffic, canceled plans, or a deadline lingering over your head like a blinking LED. As annoying as these things are, you can only control so much.

Let's take control of what we can, shall we?

Instead of getting caught up in things that didn't go as planned, begin to restore your peace by making time for yourself and using it wisely.

In *The Get A Life Campaign,* Dr. Tyeese Gaines tells us we have to take our lives back, even if you have to squeeze free time into an impossible schedule. Despite the demands on our time and energy, finding a meditative moment is one way to refocus your mind and to let go of things not in your control.

LET'S RECLAIM THE MOMENT.
Breathe in while counting to three.
Breathe out and count to six.
Repeat. Feel free to close your eyes this time.

When life brings stressful circumstances, take those eighteen seconds or more to center yourself and then proceed with your checklist in order of priority, one task at a time. The Mayo Clinic says meditation is a simple, fast way to reduce the day's stress. It really is as I meditate a few times a week for only five minutes. (Mayo Clinic Staff, 2020)

The *HuffPost* featured an article highlighting the "I get to" mentality instead of an "I have to" mindset. (RYOT Studio, 2019) When I meditate, I am reminded of the opportunities I have been given and the choices I have to take control of my life every day. Having much to do is exhausting, and to think a few intentional breaths a day helps reduce the stress is magical. We tend to think of our "to-do" lists and opportunities as stressful occurrences when in fact we *get to* do these things and have the capacity and means to experience them.

Take childrearing. I've had the privilege of raising my brother since age ten, becoming his legal guardian when I was twenty-three years old. From figuring out my professional next steps, securing enough funds for childcare and food, helping my brother reshape his habits, among several other tasks (big and small), I had to find an outlet to remind myself that I was not failing as a caregiver.

Fitness training and meditation helped me find comfort in raising my brother the best way I knew how and to be proud that *I get to* witness the incredible young man he is.

Taking a moment to calm your mind and focus on the things you get to do will hopefully make for a more joyous accomplishment. The deadline will eventually come and go, and the project will be done!

MOMENT OF REFLECTION:
"If you want to conquer the anxiety of life, live in the moment, live in the breath."

—AMIT RAY

WEEKLY TO-DO:
Challenge yourself to practice the breathing technique when the day or moment feels overwhelming. Go on for as long as needed to regain your focus and to remind yourself of what you get to do instead of what you have to do.

WEEK 22

SAY NO

―

*"You have a right to say no. Most of us have very weak and flaccid **no** muscles. We feel guilty for saying no. We get ostracized and challenged for saying no, so we forget it's our choice. Your **no** muscle has to be built up to get to a place where you can say, I don't care if that's what you want. I don't want that. **No**."*
—IYANLA VANZANT

This meeting meant more than just the forty minutes scheduled for it; I had the privilege of working with two colleagues to carry our organization's research forward. My boss tried to take that space away, not knowing how important it was to my leadership development. I mustered up the courage to tell my boss, "No, I will not cancel this meeting." She respected my stern decline, and we had a brief conversation about why, which went much better than I anticipated. I expressed my concern to the person who approved my salary, and I couldn't believe how empowering it was.

One of the hardest things to do for many of us is to say no. Something will likely always require too much time and energy. Even though we may care, the time we'll have to sacrifice or magically find in our schedule doesn't always seem worthwhile. We are so used to doing our best to squeeze in opportunities and experiences that we forget to consider "free" time in our schedules as a benefit *and* a necessity.

On average, we have about eight solid hours any given day to do additional things outside of sleep, work or school, and standing commitments. Those precious eight hours could be spent working on your side business, spending time with loved ones, exercising, watching your favorite show, and more—the point here is that *you* get to decide how to spend that time and do exactly what you want to do instead of being held hostage by what others want you to do.

Saying yes to everything is not a badge of honor and agreeing to participate in too many activities can be bad for your health. According to Jodi Clarke, licensed professional counselor and mental health service provider, "Being overly busy and exhausted may lead to an increase in stress and/or decreased self-esteem. This may trigger more serious mental health disorders including anxiety disorders, depression, and substance use disorders." The potential impact on our health due to taking on too many responsibilities requires self-intervention; it is important to consider to whom we say yes to, what we agree to, and why we agree to it. (Clarke, 2021)

Your *yeses* should reflect your absolute interest and desire to participate, and you should not feel forced. Telling my boss "no" was tough, but keeping those meetings on the calendar benefited the organization's research much more than it would have without it.

So, for the next wedding invitation that you have no desire to RSVP for or project you do not have the capacity to work on, flex your *no* muscle!

MOMENT OF REFLECTION:
"Saying no can be the ultimate self-care."
—CLAUDIA BLACK

WEEKLY TO-DO:
Challenge yourself this week to say no to at least one invitation, event, or ask, and more importantly, practice not explaining *why* you said no. Often, we get defensive and feel like we need to justify to everyone why we want our free time. You do not owe anyone a detailed explanation. If saying no outright is a bit challenging, try "No thank you, but I appreciate the invitation," "I am going to pass on this invitation, but please keep me in mind for the next one," or "It is very kind of you to invite me though I have a prior commitment, but thank you."

WEEK 23

ASK THE QUESTION

"He who asks a question remains a fool for five minutes. He who does not ask, remains a fool forever."

—CHINESE PROVERB

I failed my driving test on my first try. It was three days before my twenty-first birthday. I was devastated. My friend let me take her car out for a few spins, and I was confident that I could drive like an expert…until the driving test instructor made me parallel park. I learned to drive in New York City and practiced in Washington, DC, and I never asked for help with parallel parking. The irony!

Looking back, failing the driving test that day taught me two lessons:

1. ask specific questions to avoid preventable mistakes.
2. time is expensive so don't waste it.

The fear of asking too many questions upfront can lead to unanticipated outcomes. Try not to assume you know what you are doing; it's better to ask seemingly obvious questions than to get to the end of an assignment just to start over again.

Once, I completed an entire statistical analysis for a project, just to have my boss tell me that was not the direction she wanted to go. If only I had asked every question I could think of before starting the analysis, I would have saved fifteen hours of my life and would not have had to restart the analysis.

As a summer camp counselor used to say to me, "No question is a dumb question."

According to the Wharton School of the University of Pennsylvania, most people actually don't mind being asked questions and asking them does not leave a bad impression. In an interview about their paper "The (Better Than Expected) Consequences of Asking Sensitive Questions," researchers Einav Hart, Eric VanEpps, and Maurice Schweitzer discussed the value of asking sensitive questions. (Schweitzer, 2021)

"If I ask a very technical question or a very specific question, it can demonstrate that I'm prepared or that I really know my field or I know the intricacies of what we're talking about. We can reveal important information, or information about our assumptions through the questions that we ask," says Maurice Schweitzer, who is also a negotiations professor at the Wharton School of Business at the University of Pennsylvania.

I remind my younger brother of the consequence of not asking questions often in school. Just like most younger brothers, advice goes in one ear and out the other—he barely asks his teachers such simple questions.

So, the possible solution here is to ask ourselves, *How do we establish a working relationship with others and in situations where we can feel comfortable enough to ask necessary questions that will move us forward*? You can probably think of a handful of questions that need to be asked, whether it is about your job or how to move your career further along.

It all starts with a question:

- "Can you help me understand this a bit more?"
- "I'm unsure of how this may go. Can you explain this to me in more detail please?"
- "How would you prefer or recommend I move forward?"

The questions are endless! You just have to ask.

Going about life with unanswered questions can leave you dissatisfied with its course. The answer on the other side may not be what you wanted or expected, but at least you know the answer. The answer may even be better than what you expected! So, when it comes to asking questions, regardless of how it may sound or come out, in the words of Nike, "Just do it!"

MOMENT OF REFLECTION:

"Questions focus our thinking. Ask empowering questions like: What's good about this? What's not perfect about it yet? What am I going to do next time? How can I do this and have fun doing it?"

—CHARLES CONNOLLY

WEEKLY TO-DO:

Whenever you feel the urge to resist following up on a conversation, request, or situation this week, challenge yourself to ask at least two follow up questions. Write down the questions beforehand if you need to; just make sure to ask them. How did asking the question make you feel? Did you get the answer(s) you anticipated?

WEEK 24

ELIMINATE WHAT DOESN'T HELP YOU EVOLVE

―

"In the never-ending battle between order and chaos, clutter sides with chaos every time. Anything that you possess that does not add to your life or your happiness eventually becomes a burden."

—JOHN ROBBINS

If you are obsessed with Marie Kondo, star of Netflix's *Tidying Up with Marie Kondo*, you already understand how refreshing it is to observe others rid their personal spaces of clutter.

Watching people donate old jeans and the collection of forks sitting in boxes untouched can be incredibly freeing even for the viewer. Donating sentimental items are the worst because people tend to hold on to these items for way too long, and deep down they have no use anymore.

If you're not familiar with Kondo's tidying phenomenon, dubbed the KonMari Method™, it suggests that to begin tidying you should start with clothes, then books, papers, komono (miscellaneous items), and finally the sentimental items. Talk about saving the best for last—sarcasm intended.

Removing clutter can help people navigate their spaces with ease and open the mental space to pursue more improvements in their lives. In Kondo's words, "Tidying is the act of confronting yourself."

Carrying around clutter, literally and figuratively, can hold us back. We often think of clutter in the physical sense, but it is also bad habits, irrational behaviors, outdated ideas, and toxic relationships.

I dated someone while in college who did not have access to the new experiences I was being introduced to. He was working part time and didn't have the social life that comes with attending college. He gradually expressed envy and disdain toward my having new friends, getting excited about topics discussed in class, and even trying different cuisine. The guilt I felt became mental clutter, and I was unable to embrace and enjoy my new opportunities.

When we have opportunities that will impact our lives, it is important that we do not compromise on becoming a more improved version of ourselves—even if it takes breaking up. The lives we are capable of influencing and changing for the better relies on our ability to move aside the people, habits, ideas, and behaviors that will get in the way.

The next time you discover something that doesn't contribute to your evolution, kindly tell it "No, thank you" and keep pressing forward, even if it's tempting to indulge yourself in it.

MOMENT OF REFLECTION:
"You can't reach for anything new if your hands are still full of yesterday's junk."
—LOUISE SMITH

WEEKLY TO-DO:
What is keeping you from becoming the best version of yourself? Is it a habit or relationship? Is it a behavior or idea? Take some time this week to tidy up clutter that's been getting in your way of success. Consider discussing this with a trusted friend or loved one about what might be impacting your self-growth and ask them for strategies to help you eliminate it.

WEEK 25

YOU MATTER MORE

"It's not selfish, but selfless to be first, to be as good as possible to you, to take care of you, to keep you whole and healthy, that doesn't mean that you disregard everything and everyone, but you gotta keep your cup full."

—IYANLA VANZANT

Even in a lifelong relationship, there has to be balance—the balance of a stable partnership, family and other responsibilities, and most importantly, yourself. Yes, *you*; balance *your* wellness first before all else.

Putting yourself first seems easy enough, until every responsibility becomes your responsibility. The fear of everything falling apart becomes an excuse for why you have to keep showing up all the time. While trying to balance everything, we neglect our own well-being. When we neglect our wellness, we destabilize the very pedestal that everything and everyone relies on—*ourselves*.

I learned this lesson the hard way. Two weeks before my then ten-year-old brother permanently moved in with me, I was extremely stressed and anxious about making sure our living situation was perfect. I was told that someone from social services would inspect every room of our soon-to-be home to make sure it was safe and "livable."

I took out credit cards to purchase furniture, filled the cabinets and refrigerator with food, and secured additional necessities to show I was capable of caring for him. I became so overwhelmed by the financial stress and the looming social worker visit that I passed out at work in front of my colleagues, resulting in an overnight stay in the hospital.

This health scare taught me two major lessons:

1. Ask for help. After leaving the hospital, I contacted a trusted loved one to ask if they could help me obtain the remaining resources needed for my brother's arrival. Had I done this earlier, it would have alleviated stress and anxiety during this time.
2. Parenting is hard. I did not know much about raising a child, since I was still "raising" myself.

It is impossible to give without sacrificing part of ourselves in return. In my case, my mental and physical health took the brunt of it.

It is critical to recognize that when you put yourself first, you will have the strength, motivation, perspective, and time to balance additional responsibilities and to discern when to take something off your plate. It is also critical to say *no* and to ask for help to preserve your well-being and to resist the notion that if only you can do everything you will be perfect.

Unfortunately, perfection comes at its own costs. Choose to do things in ways most natural and fitting for you and adjust if you think it is reasonably necessary. If you don't want to do something, don't. If it doesn't feel good, stop. If it is bothering you, speak up. The more you bottle up inside you, the more you will become like a steaming pot. Unfortunately, it may be your significant other, your children, your friends, or your younger sibling who will be impacted by it.

Remember this: When life becomes too difficult to balance, be it children, schoolwork, relationships, finances, etc., always choose what is best for you in the moment, release control, and start asking for help and releasing responsibility antithetical to putting you first.

MOMENT OF REFLECTION:
"You always have to remember to take care of you first and foremost; because when you stop taking care of yourself, you get out of balance, and you really forget how to take care of others."

—JADA PINKETT SMITH

WEEKLY TO-DO:
Choose one day this week to commit to only doing something for yourself. Pick an activity that brings you joy, relaxation, and peace. Schedule the day and time(s) in your calendar, and make sure to plan your day accordingly and responsibly.

WEEK 26

TAKE THE DAY OFF

———

"Each person deserves a day away in which no problems are confronted, no solutions searched for. Each of us needs to withdraw from the cares which will not withdraw from us."

—MAYA ANGELOU

Before we were married, my partner and I were walking to a restaurant for lunch, and I went to the bathroom on myself. Yup, you read that correctly. The sad thing is, I realized what happened a bit too late.

I immediately stopped walking when I felt dampness on my calves, and my partner knew something was wrong. I told him what just happened, and we slowly turned around to go back to my apartment. I was extremely embarrassed, but all I could do was shower, change, and apologize profusely through tears. He hugged me and told me everything would be fine and to relax.

Ironically, we were walking to lunch so I could relax and to get some fresh air. I was dealing with family and work stress that day, and he was eager to treat me to a nice lunch to help me calm down. In hindsight, I should have just called out of work.

I know that my situation was a bit TMI, but I share this to emphasize that physical and mental exhaustion have very real ramifications and they can manifest in different ways. I had become so riddled with stress that my body literally demanded me to sit down and be still. My stubbornness always ignored these demands to the point where my body started shouting at me in the form of migraines, muscle aches, restlessness, loss of appetite, and even incontinence—all in my mid-twenties.

If you have been here before in some fashion, you know what could have been an "hour a day" relaxation or mindfulness regimen becomes a three-day physical and mental shutdown. If you have not been here before, then please learn from my mistakes so you can avoid such a painful experience.

You may now be asking yourself, "How can I prevent this from happening to me?" Plainly, *take the day off*! When your responsibilities call, they may require tasks that must be done right now, pronto! But what happens if your body shuts down like mine did and now you are out of commission for three days? "Right now" isn't quite immediate any longer. One relaxing day-off seems more reasonable than three incapacitated days off. Trust me, your world will remain on its axis.

McLean Hospital, a Harvard Medical School Affiliate, acknowledges that even though taking a day off has positive effects, many people do not take them out of fear of appearing weak, unable to balance daily pressures, or thought of as having a mental illness. In addition to the guidance that McLean Hospital provides to maximize the benefits of taking a "mental health day," please do not internalize company, organizational, or family culture that does not respect your personal health and wellness. According to McLean's Dr. Andrew M. Kuller, PsyD, ABPP, "The goal of a mental health day is to clarify what your values are and try to bring your day in line with those values so you can get back on track."

Taking a day off to get back on track shouldn't just be a wish; it should be a goal. If you work, use some accrued time off and ask a coworker or your supervisor if you can add them as a contact person in your "out of office" email reply.

If you are a student, email your professors and inform them of your absence. If they ask why, tell them you are taking a "restorative day" or a "mental health day." If you are a freelancer or contractor, inform your clients you will be unavailable for a day, and you'll be back in touch in twenty-four to forty-eight hours.

If you are a parent with small children, work with your partner, hire a sitter, or ask a trusted loved one to look after your children while you take a "restorative day." Wherever you are, make the appropriate arrangements to take your day. If you are able, take another one (in my best DJ Khaled voice)!

Do whatever you truly want to do on that day that will bring you peace, joy, and refreshment. Taking a day off is necessary and it's not an if, but when. A good rule of thumb is to plan and communicate ahead if possible.

MOMENT OF REFLECTION:

"Your calm mind is the ultimate weapon against your challenges. So, relax."

—BRYANT MCGILL

WEEKLY TO-DO:

Choose a day this month when you will take off, and begin planning for your day (for example, requesting time off, finding and hiring a sitter, picking your book to read, reserving a spa day (it can be DIY!) or hotel stay, etc.) this weekend. Block the day off on your calendar(s) and commit to taking that day off, despite what may come up (unless there is an absolute emergency!).

WEEK 27

BE FLEXIBLE

"Life is movement. The more life there is, the more flexibility there is. The more fluid you are, the more you are alive."
—ARNAUD DESJARDINS

There is nothing like a sense of security. You've developed a routine that is pretty much the same every day, more or less.

But what if this sense of security challenges your desire to break from your "everyday" to explore opportunities that may be more fulfilling? If this question has you contemplating your life decisions now, fabulous!

As a former aspiring fiction writer, Tayvia Pierce's stagnancy at her administrative job created a personal void in her career as a writer. In our interview, she shared that deep down she wanted to write full time as a fiction author, but the security in having a stable job to provide for her children and home needs was necessary. Tayvia found comfort in doing her administrative job well, though there wasn't much room for professional growth. Instead of leaving her job to pursue a career as a fiction author, she remained at her job for years.

Unfortunately, the flexibility to leave a job or opportunity when you have to maintain a household can seem impossible. Even when your instincts tell you to follow your desires, the rational voice in your head tells you to do the complete opposite. For Tayvia, she remained in her administrative role because of its stability until she was laid off from work unexpectedly.

Sometimes the universe has a way with giving you exactly what you want. As infuriating as getting laid off can be, especially when your next opportunity is uncertain; for Tayvia it forced her to take control over the situation immediately. Suddenly, she was free from a job she perceived as safe and secure.

"It was actually one of the best things that could have happened to me," Tayvia mentioned about being laid off. She was able to breathe, find clarity, and take control over the path she truly wanted to be on. This step "backward" was the spring that propelled Tayvia forward to designing her life around the things she cared most about and into her dream job. She is now a full-time writer and the author of the *Rise of the Phoenix* fiction book series.

Find the freedom to do what you love and design your life around the things you care about. Having opportunities—whether they are jobs or relationships—that offer securities aren't bad things, but they can also lead to dissatisfaction and feeling stuck.

Also, find the courage to plunge into the unknown. Knowing you have the flexibility to choose where you want to be and what you want to do is key to living the life you deserve. The uncertainty you feel about the unknown is normal, but that feeling should not be the reason not to try experiences for which you can't predict the outcome.

Challenge the irrational voice in your head and take that leap of faith. Yes, leaps of faith should be paired with a strategy if you have time to develop one but be confident that an awesome opportunity on the other side awaits you.

MOMENT OF REFLECTION:
"Flexibility makes buildings to be stronger, imagine what it can do to your soul."

—CARLOS BARRIOS

WEEKLY TO-DO:
What are your life's non-negotiables? Are you more or less flexible when it comes to these things? Take thirty minutes this week to reflect on how you have been designing your life around your flexibilities or the lack thereof.

WEEK 28

CHECK YOUR PRIORITIES

"A simple life is not seeing how little we can get by with – that's poverty – but how efficiently we can put first things first. When you're clear about your purpose and your priorities, you can painlessly discard whatever does not support these, whether it's clutter in your cabinets or commitments on your calendar."
—VICTORIA MORAN

You have a lot going on.

There's so much to get done with so little time. If you are anything like me, you are going to make sure everything is completed at the expense of your social life and well-being. However, making such sacrifices can have long-term implications on your well-being. It may not seem like a big sacrifice now, but down the road your schedule may lead to "borderline burnout."

While "borderline burnout" isn't a clinical term, I use it to describe the feeling of juggling work, parenting, school, marriage, home responsibilities, and side hustles. Burnout, its clinical counterpart, describes the consequences of severe stress that results from working under prolonged pressures. (InformedHealth.org, 2020)

The difference between "borderline burnout" and burnout is the level of severity; borderline burnout is the feeling of fatigue and being overwhelmed under pressure while remaining mentally and physically functional. The sudden urge to binge-watch a Netflix series and eat ice cream is a clear sign for me that "borderline burnout" is nearing. Does this urge sound familiar?

A self-imposed breakdown can be prevented with the help of rearranging priorities. Try not to quickly assign all your responsibilities as urgent; instead, list your three must-dos in levels of importance, get those done, then complete the other tasks if you're up for it.

I am reminded of Tom Bilyeu's interview with Lisa Nichols, a motivational speaker, author, and founder and CEO of Motivating the Masses, Inc. (Bilyeu, 2016) She elaborated on how she chose to shift her lived experiences to reflect the life she imagined for herself and her son. Amid navigating public assistance in South Central Los Angeles and single parenting after her son's father went to prison, she said the keys to her success were "relocating her mind, relocating her body, relocating her finances, relocating her possibilities, and relocating her son's future."

Through utilizing resources at work and networking opportunities, Nichols made intentional decisions to learn all she could from asking questions, researching, and saving money. She wrote herself a check for a manageable amount every pay period for three and a half years with the memo, "Funding my dream," without having an actual dream in mind.

After three and a half years of saving, she checked her account to discover she had saved over $60,000, way more money than she ever had in her life.

This money changed her life. Nichols moved out of public housing, wrote and published a book, and founded her company. She's now a *New York Times* best-selling author, transformational coach, philanthropist, and one of two Black women with a business on Wall Street.

Lisa Nichols' journey is the epitome of "get your priorities in check." She shared a quote from her grandmother that sums it all up: "Your conviction and your convenience do not live on the same block." In other words, what you want out of life and where you are now don't go together well.

It starts with leveling your priorities and making room for your own growth, sanity, and happiness.

MOMENT OF REFLECTION:
"It's not what's happening to you now or what has happened in your past that determines who you become. Rather, it's your decisions about what to focus on, what things mean to you, and what you're going to do about them that will determine your ultimate destiny."
—ANTHONY ROBBINS

WEEKLY TO-DO:
What three things bring you joy? What three things drain you but are not critical? Add an additional hour to your schedule this week to something that brings you joy and subtract an hour from something that drains you but isn't critical.

WEEK 29

DREAM REAL BIG

"The size of your dreams must always exceed your current capacity to achieve them. If your dreams don't scare you, they aren't big enough."

—ELLEN JOHNSON SIRLEAF

I gifted myself a stethoscope when I was accepted into medical school. But when it arrived and I put it around my neck while looking in the mirror, I couldn't find the courage to look at myself wearing it. I didn't understand why I couldn't do it! I'd worked *so* hard to see myself as a physician, and when I looked in the mirror, I was unnerved by the reflection looking back at me.

Honestly, this experience scared and excited me at the same time. Looking back, I was scared because the thought of people's lives in my hands felt unreal. I knew I needed to confront my fear of seeing myself as a medical student in small doses to help avoid becoming overwhelmed by its reality.

Now imagine, you—yes *you!*—doing the one thing you've always wanted to do. Commit to realizing that feeling! Every day you should take at least one step toward accomplishing that goal knowing that you're a step closer than you were the day before. No need to complain about how long it will take; the time will pass anyhow, so you might as well spend it progressing toward your goal. Take the time you need. Just don't stop!

With all the obstacles it took me to get to this point, from graduating college, taking organic chemistry four times, and fearing getting into medical school would take several more years, it's unbelievable I will actually get to wear *my* stethoscope.

My motivation to keep going stemmed from the thought of what I could be doing to help communities fight health disparities. It will always bother me to see communities suffering from preventable health conditions, like Type 2 diabetes and obesity.

My family has struggled with preventable health conditions for years, and it is a circumstance I have grappled with since childhood. What I envision myself doing for my family and what I imagine for thousands of others is to provide the care and resources they deserve to live healthy and fulfilling lives.

My dream of becoming a physician that once felt like a mountain is now a firm landing, standing hand in hand with others with fervor for healthier communities. And even at the "top," it's still hard to breathe. I am on my way to being the doctor the world and my community needs.

Keep climbing. Look at yourself in the mirror and tell yourself who you are and who you will be. Affirm your dream and keep pressing forward until it's a reality.

MOMENT OF REFLECTION:
"If you can't fly then run, if you can't run then walk, if you can't walk then crawl, but whatever you do you have to keep moving forward."
—DR. MARTIN LUTHER KING, JR.

WEEKLY TO-DO:
Think about a loved one or friend who has been on their life journey for some time, whether they have accomplished their dream. Contact them this weekend, share that you were thinking of them, and wish them well on their continued journey. If you're up to it, ask them if they wouldn't mind being your accountability partner while you move forward toward your dream. Having someone to talk to about your journey helps you stay on track.

WEEK 30

CHOOSE ACTION OVER ANGER

"The time is always right to do what is right."
—DR. MARTIN LUTHER KING, JR.

Something is likely to piss you off if it hasn't already. You'll go through stages of emotions, thoughts, and reactions because you're upset. Your feelings will be valid, and it may take time to work through them. Instead of channeling those feelings into rage, consider how you can redirect that energy into something action oriented.

I've been extremely passionate about many movements and causes, but my full-time work and home responsibilities at the time didn't allow me to participate or contribute in ways I would have preferred.

The protests for Black lives in spring and summer of 2020 were particularly difficult to participate in due to the COVID-19 pandemic. My weakened immune system prevented me from marching outdoors with others, but I knew if I wanted to be present, my presence had to take on different forms. To grieve the losses of Black lives, my friends and I created a YouTube podcast called "Stuff & Things" to support one another through conversation, safe protesting, and ways of contributing.

When showing up physically is impossible or unlikely, I show up using my financial and social resources. I post to social media and send text messages and emails to loved ones to bring awareness to what's happening. I donate what I can to move the efforts forward. I speak up unapologetically about what's happening. If there is a will, there certainly is a way to contribute in some way.

When the chance to participate is impossible altogether, I talk to a trusted person about it, such as my partner, best friend, or therapist. It's easy to remain worked up about something that's out of your control, and it can have implications on your mental health.

Regardless of what you choose to do to work through your anger, make sure that you take care of you first then decide how you can show up if possible.

MOMENT OF REFLECTION:

"Anger...it's a paralyzing emotion...you can't get anything done. People sort of think it's an interesting, passionate, and igniting feeling—I don't think it's any of that—it's helpless...it's absence of control—and I need all of my skills, all of the control, all of my powers...and anger doesn't provide any of that—I have no use for it whatsoever."

—TONI MORRISON

WEEKLY TO-DO:

Take ten minutes this week to write down how you overcame a situation that angered you. How would you have handled the situation differently?

WEEK 31

STICK TO YOUR PLAN

"Our goals can only be reached through a vehicle of a plan, in which we must fervently believe, and upon which we must vigorously act. There is no other route to success."
—PABLO PICASSO

We set out on a journey to accomplish our dreams. Every now and then, something gets in the way of us doing just that. We stress about it; we cry about it. We even think, "Should I keep moving forward? Why keep doing this when everything seems to be going against the few things I need to accomplish?"

For me, that accomplishment was becoming a physician.

Ever since I could walk, talk, and remember, I wanted to be a physician. My family's second home was the hospital because my oldest brother was frequently admitted due to his sickle cell disease. I was intrigued by how the physicians would treat my brother's pain and their kindness to me when I asked all sorts of questions about my brother's treatments.

In addition to physicians' roles at the bedside, I became curious about how doctors could be impactful in my neighborhood, Westville Manor in New Haven, Connecticut, in preventing obesity, asthma, and trauma from gun violence in its residents. My brother's care and my neighborhood's condition were early influences for why I needed to become a physician.

Unfortunately, when I went to college, my initial plan for medical school did not go as I'd expected. While in college, I needed to balance my classes and volunteer work, my family's homelessness, and my sudden need to work, which all negatively impacted my grades.

But I remained focused on my dream of becoming a physician by volunteering in communities in Washington, DC similar to my own, as well as working in clinical settings and conducting research. I even attended graduate school to study public health to complement my eventual medical career.

Seven years after graduate school and working full time, despite the unexpected hurdles, I finally got into medical school.

I share my journey often as a reminder you can still accomplish your dreams regardless of obstacles that will come your way. Maybe that obstacle for you is showing up for a job you are not passionate about, and you'd rather invest your time into your own business. Maybe it is the flexibility, stability, and security your job provides for you and your children's well-being that make taking risks seem impossible. Despite your realities, small and meaningful steps will get you closer to your dream slowly but surely.

Your incremental steps are probably more critical than your lofty ones. Running a marathon is less intimidating when you focus on going one step at a time rather than looking at all twenty-six miles at once. If you continue to move forward toward the goals that matter most to you, regardless of how long it may take, your accomplishment will be worth every bit!

MOMENT OF REFLECTION:
"Obstacles don't have to stop you. If you run into a wall, don't turn around and give up. Figure out how to climb it, go through it, or work around it."

—MICHAEL JORDAN

WEEKLY TO-DO:
Has someone ever invited you to make a vision board? If you have yet to make one, take about ten minutes this week to write down and visualize what you want your life to look like in the next two years. Select your absolute top three and devise your first draft plan to accomplish them.

WEEK 32

SURROUND YOURSELF WITH GREAT PEOPLE

―

"Walk with the dreamers, the believers, the courageous, the cheerful, the planners, the doers, the successful people with their heads in the clouds and their feet on the ground."
—WILFERD PETERSON

Ever since we were young, we were told to be careful of the friends we keep. Whether it was your parents, teacher, or mentor telling you this, you most likely knew that in some way their suggestions were for your own good.

From as long ago as I can remember, my mom used to say, "Three birds of a feather flock together," reminding me the people who I'd hang around should have similar goals, behaviors, and habits. We were to support each other, whether for good or for bad. The one thing I knew for sure is whoever I chose to spend most of my time with would become a reflection of me.

Even as an adult when I think of my mom's words, I ask myself, "*Is this person worth being around so much?*" or more truthfully, "*Do I* actually *like them as much as I think I do?*" I was cautious of the influence people would have on me.

Though I was open to friendships with those with different life experiences and beliefs than mine, if we were to be extensions of one another by association, I needed to trust we wouldn't misrepresent each other. With this in mind, I had to be somewhat strategic. My natural gravitation to certain types of people seemed to take me in a good direction, and because I was skeptical, I did not want to take these connections for granted.

Like the metaphor my mom said, I once heard we are the average of the five people we spend the most time with. In this vein, all my friends encourage me and hold me accountable. I also think an important part of friendship is reciprocity. It is a gift to have friends who genuinely want to see you win too! I encourage you to surround yourself with similar people. Your five closest friends should bring positivity into your life.

Others who you decide to surround yourself by should bring positivity as well. They can be your intimate partner, a professor, a mentor, etc. Consider if your close friends value your friendship before offering too much of your hard-earned money or time. If they are reaching for the stars and you are trailing behind them, make sure you can contribute your part to their success so as they go farther, you can go farther, too.

Please do not sacrifice the great things you've been working so hard to achieve due to the influence of people you spend the most time with.

MOMENT OF REFLECTION:
"Stop making yourself small so others can feel big."
—TARA JAYE FRANK

WEEKLY TO-DO:
Take ten minutes this week to make a list of the people you spend most of your time with. Next to their names, in under ten words, write down how they contribute to your current success. After you've made your list, take five minutes to reflect on how you feel about your responses.

WEEK 33

IT'S OK TO CRY

"Cry. Forgive. Learn. Move on. Let your tears water the seeds of your future happiness."
—STEVE MARABOLI

"Encourage Yourself" by Donald Lawrence and The Tri-City Singers is the one song that takes me on an emotional rollercoaster. The first two verses remind me it is important to encourage myself and speak victory out loud when I experience hardships. This occasional reminder triggers soul-cleansing tears, and afterward I feel like I can conquer the world.

When I hear this song or in any situation when I feel the urge, I give myself permission to cry because it is incredibly freeing. I cry when my friends get new jobs, when my younger brothers take my advice seriously, or even when I am unsure about the outcome of an exam.

Whether it's a few tears or I'm crying a river, I believe that if the urge is there your tears deserve to be released.

Releasing tears allows the weight of struggles or of overwhelming joy to lift from my shoulders. A good cry sometimes makes me want to cry more, much like an emotional domino effect. Afterward, my mental and physical well-being recharges, my thoughts are clearer, and my decisions are firm.

So many of us are embarrassed to *feel* or allow others to witness our emotions, though expressing emotions doesn't make us weak. You do not need to apologize or resist; your feelings are valid. When you give yourself permission to emote, with practice you lower the risk of overexpressing in unwelcome spaces.

While overexpressing isn't necessarily damaging, it can cloud your thoughts and perspectives, like trying to drive with a foggy windshield!

If you have difficulty in expressing your feelings or overexpressing is getting in the way of relationships and opportunities, I recommend talking to a therapist or counselor. A therapist or counselor can help you develop ways to cope and express emotions in a safe and valuable way.

Free yourself from yourself! When your spirit moves, close your eyes, feel all you are feeling, and cry if you must. Also, give yourself permission to have emotional support whose shoulder is yours to cry on.

MOMENT OF REFLECTION:
"I gave myself permission to feel and experience all of my emotions. In order to do that, I had to stop being afraid to feel. In order to do that, I taught myself to believe that no matter what I felt or what happened when I felt it, I would be okay."
—IYANLA VANZANT

WEEKLY TO-DO:
Schedule "free time" this week for fifteen to thirty minutes to check in with yourself, literally. Find a comfortable space—on the couch, floor, bed, car, etc.—close your eyes and think about how you feel in the moment. Consider if your feelings are affecting your goals, relationships, productivity, or other things. After you've checked in with yourself, treat yourself to something you like!

WEEK 34

PLAN ACCORDINGLY

"Give me six hours to chop down a tree and I will spend the first four sharpening the axe."

—ABRAHAM LINCOLN

Did you go to school, graduate, and then immediately expect a well-paying job? In the United States, graduates learn that earning a degree may not be enough to secure a good job. (Singletary, 2019) While you may have taken the "right" path by first earning your degree, figuring out how to make the degree work for you takes a little more planning.

Like earning a degree, I and others I know also set out to accomplish goals the "right way," paths often influenced by our parents, social circles, or societal expectations. We earn degrees, aim to find the perfect spouse, have children and a dog, and the big house with a white picket fence, often in this order.

Unfortunately, the order of life rarely works out as anticipated. As a result, we obsess over a path that will give us the outcome we desire, or we take a different route altogether.

The direction you choose to go down should be strategic, well thought out, and the route *you* want to take regardless of its level of difficulty.

Decide the best path for yourself that does not compromise on rigor, or the skills-building needed to make sure you are well prepared. Paying off debt is a good example. Dave Ramsey's debt snowball plan is a strategy I have personally used to pay off credit card debt and is a general concept I use to think about my life's plan. (Ramsey Solutions, 2021)

Dave Ramsey instructs those who are paying off debt to tackle the smallest debt first. This strategy calls for listing all your debts from least to greatest, and once you have paid off the smallest debt you roll the same amount over that you allocated for the smallest debt and add it to the next smaller debt to repay. It is more manageable to pay off the smaller debt and to check them off your list as you go. (Ramsey Solutions, 2021)

Just as Ramsey suggests starting small, plan short-term goals first. Once you've checked off one, you will be eager and motivated to check off the next. Various short-term goals include finishing a degree program you started years ago, buying the home you started searching for, or getting the job you've always hoped for.

Writing a checklist of things you want to achieve from easiest to difficult enables you to plan your methods of attack with more confidence. Trying to do everything at once can become so complicated that you wind up getting nothing done.

I accumulated $20,000 in credit card debt over two years as I tried to pay down all four cards at once. The interest rates for the credit cards were between 15 percent and 26 percent, so the minimum payments did not bring down the balances at all. It got to the point where I felt as if I were drowning because all my leftover income from my paychecks went to credit debt.

With no additional funds to save or to have a social life, I had to figure out a way to balance *and* get rid my debt. My work colleague introduced me to the Ramsey method, and I was relieved when the method finally started working for me. The plan I created using the Ramsey method worked best for me. I paid off my credit debt in a little over a year.

With that said, the "right way" is whichever way that works best for you to achieve your goal. It's helpful to try suggested plans and methods to land on the one most effective for you. You can secure the perfect, well-paying job or pay down your debt by checking off a few boxes one at a time!

MOMENT OF REFLECTION:
"Have a bias toward action—let's see something happen now. You can break that big plan into small steps and take the first step right away."

—INDIRA GANDHI

WEEKLY TO-DO:
Take ten minutes to do one of two things:

1. Every day this week, begin with making a short list starting with your easiest tasks to your more time-consuming tasks. Try your best to check off all the boxes on your lists for each day, and at the end of seven days add the number of tasks you completed. Reflect on how you feel.
2. List your goals from the goal that takes the shortest time to accomplish to the goal that takes the longest time to accomplish. Pick the goal with the shortest time to accomplish and start your research to get it done.

WEEK 35

LEAN INTO YOUR IDENTITIES

―

Owning our story and loving ourselves through that process is the bravest thing that we'll ever do.
—BRENÉ BROWN

"It's time to move on because shame is destructive—and if not dealt with, it can destroy everything in its path," Tony and Emmy award-winning actor Billy Porter declared when he disclosed his HIV positive status in his 2021 interview with *The Hollywood Reporter*. Porter kept his HIV status a secret for over a decade due to fear the people would shame him and his family.

Porter no longer wanted to live behind a mask; he chose to enter his next phase of his life and career shamelessly himself.

"Having lived through the plague, my question was always, 'Why was I spared? Why am I living?' Well, I'm living so that

I can tell the story. There's a whole generation that was here, and I stand on their shoulders. I can be who I am in this space, at this time, because of the legacy they left for me. So, it's time to put my big boy pants on and talk," said Porter in the interview. This, and a series of life-changing events, led to him finally speaking out about his HIV status.

> *It was 2007, the worst year of my life. I was on the precipice of obscurity for about a decade or so, but 2007 was the worst of it. By February, I had been diagnosed with type 2 diabetes. By March, I signed bankruptcy papers. And by June, I was diagnosed HIV-positive. The shame of that time compounded with the shame that had already [accumulated] in my life silenced me, and I have lived with that shame in silence for fourteen years. HIV-positive, where I come from, growing up in the Pentecostal church with a very religious family, is God's punishment. (Porter, 2021)*

Porter's experience illustrates it is really hard to love what you do and who you are while suppressing parts of yourself that keep you moving forward. Porter feared the stigma his identities would bring, yet he leaned in with courage—he owned his story out loud. His HIV status does not define him as it is part of who he is.

Showing up unapologetically is easier for some than for others. For women in male-dominated spaces, people of color in majority white spaces, people with disabilities in primarily non-disabled places, and people who present their gender, interests, and perspectives differently than others in any space, finding the courage to accept our identities is something many of us deal with on a regular basis.

The media and historically rooted biases influence how certain groups are perceived and are treated, especially in the workforce and in schools. Such perceptions make it difficult to fully embrace oneself and inadvertently cause people to mask who they really are.

Continue to love yourself and lean into your identities. Other people's opinion is just their opinion and stems from their own lives and has no bearing on you. Wear what you want. Eat what you want. Have pride in where you are from and the skin you're in.

If you find yourself in an industry or among people who stigmatize or do not accept your identities, create your own spaces. For instance, Adaptive Sports by Move United gives young people with disabilities opportunities to play sports. Tyler Perry Studios gives Black actors and actresses opportunities to be cast and lead major roles that share Black stories. Having experienced hardships of his own in entertainment, among countless Black actors, actresses, filmmakers, directors and producers, Tyler Perry created his own way forward in the industry. (Harris, 2019)

If you find yourself doubtful, channel Billy Porter's courage and confidence. If a space denies you, the space doesn't deserve you. The *real* you will always be the best you, and your *best* you should always be present.

MOMENT OF REFLECTION:

"Love yourself...enough to take the actions required for your happiness...enough to cut yourself loose from the drama-filled past...enough to set a high standard for relationships...enough to feed your mind and body in a healthy manner...enough to forgive yourself...enough to move on."

—STEVE MARABOLI

WEEKLY TO-DO:

Which of your identities are important to you? Do you show up proud of who you are? Take thirty minutes this week to journal about your experiences when you were able to be unapologetically yourself. If what you journal about feels right, give yourself the opportunity this week to show up embracing all of you.

WEEK 36

WRITE OUT THE VISION

"If you set goals and go after them with all the determination you can muster, your gifts will take you places that will amaze you."

—LES BROWN

If you've ever played a sport, especially one like soccer, basketball, or football, you know the winner is decided by one important task—scoring. If your team scores more goals than the other team, you win. It's that simple. But as we know, the will to win goes far beyond the court itself.

Most seasoned coaches would say a good team is made up of players who have the will to win and demonstrate teamwork. My high school basketball coach used to say playing a successful game comes down to each of us players having heart, keeping our heads in the game, and executing the plays.

Running a play is an organized way of outmaneuvering the opposing team to score. These visualizations are critical because if the players haven't practiced or memorized the play when it is time to run it, it will look like a bunch of people on a field running without a plan, hoping and wishing that somehow, they will score, or a miracle will happen.

Much like on-court play, organizing our everyday lives for effective execution is a good approach to planning our future. Consider visualizing how you intend to succeed regularly, and not just for when you are "in the game."

Experts say that not only is visualization important, but it can also improve motivation, coordination, and concentration, while reducing fear and anxiety about the goal. (Niles, 2011) I used this strategy when I envisioned my first visit to Europe.

My cousin and I have talked about going to England and France since we were about ten years old. We talked about climbing the stairs of the Eiffel Tower wearing our berets, exploring castles pretending to be royals, and skipping in the streets of London. Traveling to Europe seemed out of reach coming from our poor neighborhood. After fifteen years of thinking, dreaming, and imagining, I bought a flight ticket to England and traveled to France, doing everything other than skipping in the streets of London. Unfortunately, my cousin was unable to come, but I look forward to going back with him (love you, Joes!).

Have you ever visualized what you'd like to accomplish in your life like my cousin and I did? Whether you have or have not, six ideas for how you can do it are by creating a vision board, a list, finding an accountability partner, journaling, mirror writing, or writing on sticky notes.

There are more approaches, but it is important you discover the best approach for you. Whichever you prefer, I assure you it will feel really good to cross that accomplished goal off your list, just like scoring the winning goal!

MOMENT OF REFLECTION:
"The thing about goals is that living without them is a lot more fun, in the short run. It seems to me, though, that the people who get things done, who lead, who grow and who make an impact...those people have goals."
—SETH GODIN

WEEKLY TO-DO:
Choose your vision approach: vision board, list, journal, sticky notes, writing on your mirror, etc. Find an hour this week to write down and/or visualize your goals. Once you feel like you have just the right number of goals, write, thumbtack, or tape them in a space you have to see every day (for example, your desk, your bathroom, your front door, the refrigerator, etc.). Consider using the following ideas to visualize your goals:

Vision board—If you haven't been to a New Year's vision board party or a random social night to cut pictures out of magazines or print visuals of how you envision your life in the present and future, you've been missing out! The images that catch your attention, whether it is a nice house, a fashion icon, a baby, or more, are pasted or taped together on a board for you to hang wherever you like. These are your goals and your efforts, and the universe will manifest them.

A list—Consider writing out a list of things you'd love to do. Your dreams and goals can become your ultimate checklist, so you can check them as you accomplish them one by one. Once everything is checked off, you can create a new list with new dreams and goals.

Accountability partner(s)—Share your dreams and goals with your closest loved ones and friends. This may seem a bit scary at first because you may not be sure how they will react, but this approach allows your loved ones to always hold you accountable to getting everything you hoped for accomplished. This is, by far, one of my favorites. Every time I attempt to embark on a professional journey off course, my family and friends will ask, "Don't you want to be a doctor? Do you not want to be a doctor anymore? Are you taking premed classes? Are you volunteering at the hospitals?" They go on and on about it, getting on every nerve unapologetically because they are invested in my success and fulfillment.

Journaling—Journaling is probably the preferred approach for many people because there's no script you must adhere to; you can write down whatever you want, how you want it. Whenever you are thinking about where you want to take your life, a journal is a private space for you to lay it all out. Maybe a couple of months or years after your entries, reread your journal and decide if you made any progress on what you wrote. Why, you might ask? To reference our sports analogy, if you go back to your old plays you may consider reusing the plays that only your teammates (aka your loved ones) know well. While the play may appear to be new to others, you are simply picking up where you left off and maybe add a little finesse to it.

Mirror writing—You can write your dreams and goals on your favorite mirror. Yes, your mirror, but use a dry erase marker. Your bathroom mirror may be a good place, or even your dresser mirror. The point is you will see your dreams and goals every day, multiple times a day—they will always be in your face reminding you of what you set out to accomplish. With such daily reminders, you will hopefully feel compelled to conquer them so you can finally erase them.

Sticky notes—I love sticky notes! I put them everywhere, literally making a colorful sticky paper mess. I can pick them up and stick them anywhere I need them to be so that I can see exactly what task or goal I need to complete. I also find joy in balling them up and tossing them in the trash bin once the goal is completed.

WEEK 37

BEYOND THE STATUS QUO

"Venture outside your comfort zone. To stop growing is to stop living."

—ROBIN ROBERTS

Imagine your daily routine. You most likely complete a semblance of the following: wake up, shower, brush teeth, put on work clothes, eat breakfast, then head to work, taking the usual route. All is well until unexpected traffic builds up, forcing you to get off an unfamiliar exit. Lost and frustrated, you put on your GPS for directions, and it takes you on the most scenic route to work you've ever been on.

Taking an exciting, unexpected route to work is a practical metaphor for our lives if we purposely choose to take unfamiliar paths. It is hard to get excited about something when comfort in doing the same thing all the time seems best. First, the path is familiar, so you take it out of habit. Second, you are continuing the status quo, knowing that the path will most likely remain the same over time.

This type of comfort is the definition of contentment—you are happy and satisfied with how things are. Contentment can be good but not always, especially if a suppressed fire is inside you or you have an urge to do something different or unimaginable.

At some point you've heard Rome wasn't built in a day; dreams aren't built in a day either. It takes risk-taking to defy the confines of our comfort zone.

Contentment can take away our drive to do exciting things. It seems that comfort and staying safe is our go-to, but the feeling of being free and trying new things, in itself, is thrilling.

I want you to get out and try different new things. What's the point of education, resources, support, and love from people rooting for you if you're not pushing boundaries? Those who love you aren't cheering for your mediocrity!

When I push myself to say yes to experiences, confidence overwhelms me and challenges my urge to sit still.

When my friends invited me on my first international trip to Puerto Rico, I was nervous. Visiting a place outside of the US mainland was a big deal because my mom instilled a fear in me of leaving the country due to her own fear.

I was afraid of the long flight, the language barrier, and an unfamiliar location. Despite this, I went anyway. Puerto Rico was incredible, from the food, culture, beaches, and more! It was during this trip I decided I would leave the US at least once a year. I would have never discovered my love for traveling had I stayed home.

If you have a dream or an urge to take a different route in life, go for it! Go and live your absolute best life like I did!

MOMENT OF REFLECTION:
"*Influential people are never satisfied with the status quo. They're the ones who constantly ask, 'What if?' and 'Why not?' They're not afraid to challenge conventional wisdom, and they don't disrupt things for the sake of being disruptive; they do it to make things better.*"
—TRAVIS BRADBERRY

WEEKLY TO-DO:
Intentionally changing your routine may be difficult. Every week I schedule at least one activity not on my typical schedule so I can try something different, whether that is cooking a new recipe, trying a new fitness class, or calling someone I haven't talked to in a long while. I encourage you to block off two to three hours this week to challenge your typical to-dos with something exciting that will take you out of your comfort zone.

WEEK 38

MIND YOUR BUSINESS

"Keep your attention focused entirely on what is truly your own concern, and be clear that what belongs to others is their business and none of yours."

—EPICTETUS

Many of us have a habit of worrying about what others have and what they are doing. Maybe we desire a glimpse of their life—their career, family, or their thrill for the finer things. We are constantly trying to figure out *why* they have those things and why *we* don't. Keep in mind, just because they've been presented with opportunities, items, experiences, they still may be struggling.

It is always a shift of perspective when we realize others may actually be looking at you as if your life is better than theirs; you are lucky because of the situations and experiences you have had.

A great quote I saw on Instagram said, "Don't get sidetracked by people who are not on track." You have no clue what people's journeys have been to get to where they are or what they have to endure to get to where they want to be. Similar to how you may be going through some things, your journey is where you are destined to go.

Minding your business is akin to staying in your own lane. This is not to shame you for being fascinated by what others have. It is merely a reminder you also have things going for you, even if you don't quite see them. You are on your way to being your kind of fabulous, having your kind of experiences, and loving whomever or whatever you choose to do.

You can end up wasting precious time by looking at what others have. Imagine if those fifteen minutes spent scrolling on social media was spent investing in the best version of *you*? That time could be better spent investing in your own image, figuring out how you're going to get that next step.

Stay in your own lane. Your hustle is your hustle. You'll get to where you want to go, and it starts with not worrying about what everyone else is doing, as well as not caring what other people think about what you're doing.

This is your life, and you have to live it the way you want to. It is understandable, however, that some cultural circumstances can get in the way of this, especially when family compares your track to the status quo or to others your age. Regardless of what other people are doing, *you are enough. You are worthy* of good things. *You are worthy* of opportunities—opportunities meant for *you*.

Whether your journey took off quickly or slowly, it's still part of your story. Live, love, and enjoy your life. Stay on *your* hustle. In the words of Tabitha Brown, American actress and social media personality, that's *your* business! (Bueno, 2020)

MOMENT OF REFLECTION:
"You would be very surprised with how much positive changes that you could make in your life if you could make it your top priority to mind your own business."
—EDMOND MBIAKA

WEEKLY TO-DO:
It may be time for a social media detox. If you use any social media platform, choose one day (or more) this week to refrain from using it for twenty-four hours (everything will be as you left it, I promise). Consider how to spend your time differently.

WEEK 39

TO KNOW OR NOT TO KNOW

"The public have an insatiable curiosity to know everything, except what is worth knowing."
—OSCAR WILDE

Have you ever done something that you knew from the beginning wasn't the best idea?

We've all been there— relationships we would have been better without, food that did a number on our stomachs, or jobs we took only for the salary. Should you say you knew it wasn't for you, just to discover you were right all along?

Such distractions show us that sometimes it is best to make an immediate decision. The moment we make the decision, especially if it is met with unease, prevents an arduous journey of time spent not in our best interest.

Look for a lesson in these mishaps because often they will come as a learning opportunity. Once we fully understand the lesson, our instincts help us make better immediate decisions in the future.

According to BBC, "Our gut instincts are not always as random as they seem. They can be based on a rapid appraisal of the situation. We might not always realize it, but the brain is constantly comparing our current situation with our memories of previous situations. So, when a decision feels intuitive, it might in fact be based on years of experience." (Hammond, 2019) Your past experiences created a foundation for your instincts, so the second time around when deciding on an experience is already well-informed. Even with this, you still have to consider additional insight when weighing your curiosities. (Hammond, 2019)

"Curiosity killed the cat" is a phrase my mom used to say to make the point that I learned more than I needed to, subjecting my brain to information that I would be better off not knowing. With more knowledge and experiences, we are wiser, right? Not always! According to The Phrase Finder article by Gary Martin, this phrase is described as "inquisitiveness can lead one into dangerous situations," situations that cannot be unseen or unheard.

There is still more to the phrase: "Curiosity killed the cat...*but satisfaction brought it back.*" (Martin, 2021) In other words, because you are content with knowing what it's like, you can now get back to living as you ought to.

Challenge yourself to continue taking chances, but only those you feel compelled to take. If you are really pulled in, it feels good, and you're actually curious with good insight, live your best life and share the tale on the other side.

MOMENT OF REFLECTION:
"What makes people smart, curious, alert, observant, competent, confident, resourceful, persistent—in the broadest and best sense, intelligent—is not having access to more and more learning places, resources and specialists, but being able in their lives to do a wide variety of interesting things that matter, things that challenge their ingenuity, skill, and judgement, and that make an obvious difference in their lives and the lives of the people around them."
—JOHN HOLT

WEEKLY TO-DO:
Consider an experience that you knew what going through it would be like. What would you have done differently—would you want to know, or would you rather not have known? When experiences arise this week, go with your instinct using the information and experiences you know, and reflect upon how it made a difference in your week.

WEEK 40

MAKE YOUR ___ HEALTH PRIORITY

"*He who has health has hope, and he who has hope has everything.*"

—ARABIAN PROVERB

Self-care is a buzzword these days and for good reason. Self-care is much more than lighting candles, taking a bubble bath, and retail therapy. While I enjoy all these relaxing strategies very much, I recognize other areas in my life that also deserve nurturing for a balanced life.

We are responsible for so much, and it can be difficult to find time to put ourselves first. The things we juggle can become so consuming that we neglect our mental health—work, school, family, and more. Prioritizing our short- and long-term health while balancing many tasks and responsibilities starts with a self-health check. Consider the following questions as an example.

Have you seen your primary care doctor lately? Have you reached out to a financial advisor? Where are you spiritually? When was the last time you spent time with people you love? Have your habits and behaviors as of late prompted you to consider speaking to a therapist? Are your surroundings stressing you out, requiring a change of scenery? If any of these questions have you thinking deeply about various aspects of your life, now is the time to find answers to gain optimal wellness.

As the questions above suggest, the concept of health is much broader than we tend to think and there are different types we need to consider. According to a March 2021 *World Book* article by Nayma Nishat, there are six primary types of health: physical, mental, spiritual, social, emotional, and environmental. I'd like to add an additional type of health we all are very familiar with: financial. Which type of health should you prioritize? Let's define each so you can pinpoint exactly which ones to consider further, if at all:

- Physical health—"the state of your physical body and how well it is operating." (Nishat, 2021)
- Mental health—"the psychological state of someone who is functioning at a satisfactory level of emotional and behavioral adjustment." (Nishat, 2021)
- Spiritual health—"possessing, meaning, and purpose in life; having a clear set of beliefs and living in accordance with your morals, values, and ethics." (Nishat, 2021)
- Social health—"how you get along with other people, which involves your ability to form satisfying interpersonal relationships with others." (Nishat, 2021)

- Emotional health—"a person's feelings which encompass everything about you. It actually governs all of your decisions, your mood, and who you are." (Nishat, 2021)
- Environmental health—"the field of science that studies how the environment influences human health and disease." (Nishat, 2021)
- Financial health—"measures your ability to meet your financial needs and prepare for unexpected financial emergencies." (*Self*, 2020)

Self-care matters because *you* matter.

Now that you have a better understanding of what *self-care* really means, commit to putting your health at the top of your daily to-do list.

MOMENT OF REFLECTION:
"Keep your vitality. A life without health is like a river without water."

—MAXIME LAGACÉ

WEEKLY TO-DO:
When it comes to your health, what do you need to prioritize? Choose two you can realistically make the time and effort for to improve. Take fifteen minutes this week to write down questions you have about the types of health, ways you can begin to improve your health(s), and then take an additional ten minutes to find resources that can answer your questions as soon as possible. Don't forget to contact them!

WEEK 41

CLAP FOR YOURSELF

―

"Find the love you seek, by first finding the love within yourself. Learn to rest in that place within you that is your true home."
—SRI SRI RAVI SHANKAR

Don't wait for others to celebrate you. Of course, it feels good when others show you love after an accomplishment, but let's be clear—your wins are for *you*!

Ever post something exciting to social media, in a group chat, or in a forum, and it receives very few likes or not much attention at all? If you posted something you loved and expected a good response, you probably felt a bit disappointed. You are not alone.

A 2016 study published in *Psychological Science* by Lauren Sherman and colleagues found, "The same brain circuits activated by eating chocolate and winning money are activated when teenagers see large numbers of 'likes' on their own photos or the photos of peers in a social network," findings discovered after scanning teen's brains while they used social media. (Sherman et al., 2016)

This phenomenon doesn't just occur in teens, it occurs in all of us. The release of dopamine, the neurotransmitter released when in a state of pleasure and happiness, that occurs with social media likes has an effect on one's sense of self-assurance. (Joseph, 2019) In short, the likes we receive from posts assures us what we are doing is making a difference.

The amount of information we have become comfortable with sharing is incredible. What happened to moving in silence? The World Wide Web has made access to our lives very easy, and the urge to be seen can get to the best of us.

I am guilty of this, I must admit. However, my initial intent behind creating social media profiles was to stay in touch with friends who lived internationally whom I met during a summer program. Over time, my profiles were also great for connecting with new family members and friends.

Eventually, my personal brand on social media evolved to look more professional as colleges and employers began checking. Colleges and employers checked applicants' online presence to see if they were presenting themselves well, their perception being that this was also how the applicant would reflect the institution or organization.

As such, family and friends started following my personal and professional growth more carefully. Everything, and I really mean *everything*, was cheered on, which became motivation to keep moving forward, reaching for the stars, and showing everyone I did it—whatever "it" was.

Posting publicly about my goals quickly became overwhelming, especially the question "Are you a doctor yet?" Oh, how this question would grind my gears as I worked so hard to successfully pass organic chemistry on the third *and* fourth tries! I started to move in silence at last, giving myself space to deal with my own shortcomings and to celebrate my own wins with very few people knowing.

Truthfully, it is okay if no one is checking for your wins all the time. Stepping away from questions and praise allowed me to appreciate and embrace my successes. After fasting from social media for three months, I realized that if every goal we chased was for someone else to clap, we would run the risk of suffering from stress and disappointment.

This experience taught me that whatever I am willing to share with others is actually in my control. My wins and losses are no one else's business if I decide not to share. Even with the support of friends and family along the way, the fact that I endured the hard work, sweat, and tears to accomplish my goals means that my wins belong to me.

I share my experience to make one major point—be your own audience. Take a seat, sit back, and watch your own movie. See how you've persevered through rough times. Reflect on how your strength, resilience, and commitment got you to where you are. You did that! Because you did all of it, don't wait for anyone else's claps, likes, or comments. Now give yourself a round of applause!

MOMENT OF REFLECTION:
"When you're constantly thinking of others and what they must be thinking or feeling or expecting, you wind up in this perpetual state of trying to please them. You see yourself through their eyes and you lose sight of who you are."

—MICHAEL SOLL

WEEKLY TO-DO:
Consider taking this weekend to refrain from public forums, such as social media, unless it is your work. Use this time to think about things that bring you joy, ideas or opportunities you want to work on, and spend time with or speaking to someone you love. Don't forget to celebrate yourself for any achievements this week.

WEEK 42

MORE MONEY, NEW OPPORTUNITIES

"Wealth is not about having a lot of money; it's about having a lot of options."

—CHRIS ROCK

I looked forward to every salary-based promotion at work. A decent salary increase meant I could take better vacations, improve my wardrobe, and move into a nicer apartment. In reality, my salary increases mostly went toward paying down student loans and into my savings account.

When I worked, I prioritized covering bills and basic needs, such as food, housing, and healthcare, and I lived within my means. While these immediate responsibilities are essential for most of us, it is a must that we account for our personal growth as well.

Your personal growth can include fitness, courses or certifications, branding, or just relaxing. You may not need money to engage in any of these things, but additional cash, regardless of the amount, can help move many of these activities along efficiently and more tailored to your needs.

This is where planning comes in. Try your best to figure out how much extra you *actually* have, and then decide how much you can allocate toward your goals. Bev O'Shea and Lauren Schwahn, credit and personal finance writers for NerdWallet, suggest the following budgeting techniques:

- Calculate your monthly income, pick a budgeting method, and monitor your progress.
- Try the 50/30/20 rule as a simple budgeting framework; "you spend roughly 50 percent of your after-tax dollars on necessities, no more than 30 percent on wants, and at least 20 percent on savings and debt repayment."
- Allow up to 50 percent of your income for needs.
- Leave 30 percent of your income for wants.
- Commit 20 percent of your income to savings and debt repayment.

A wise person once told me that though it's important to save for "rainy days" and to cover emergency expenses, most days are sunny. My interpretation: Be fully aware of how much money it takes to cover your needs, but do not compromise living your life and thriving in anticipation of the unknown. Make sure to make your money work for you in a way that helps you live the life you desire. But make sure you are mindful of the following:

- Basic needs
- Immediate responsibilities

- Retirement savings
- Regular savings

Now, let me share how I figured out how to buy time and tools with extra money to build the future I wanted.

When I received an increase in my salary, the additional money I earned was scheduled to go into my investment savings account every pay day. I did this because I did not want to get used to living at my means, but below my means, to save for school, house, and the comfort of knowing that I have finances to cover my needs.

Investing in yourself is always a great thing to do. Even when making sure your basics are covered, make sure to plan your wants too. Keep the 50/30/20 rule in mind when budgeting for the life you desire.

MOMENT OF REFLECTION:
"Trade money for time, not time for money. You're going to run out of time first."
—NAVAL RAVIKANT

WEEKLY TO-DO:
Take thirty minutes this week to go through your earnings and use O'Shea and Schwahn's budgeting techniques to figure out how much you truly have left over after your essentials are covered. If you are having trouble, schedule a consultation with a financial advisor or reach out to a friend who you think or know is good with saving money.

WEEK 43

STICK TO THE BASICS

"The ability to simplify means to eliminate the unnecessary so that the necessary may speak."

—HANS HOFMANN

The infamous acronym *KISS*, standing for "keep it simple stupid" or "keep it simple and straightforward," is a phrase that can be applied to just about anything. The emphasis of *KISS* is simplicity; everything we do does not require a complex plan to get it done.

I used to be the person who thought I needed to buy dozens of books or join exclusive information forums to do one thing—pass organic chemistry. [If you choose to stop reading now, I wouldn't be upset, not at all. Just pick back up next week, haha!] Yes, this class was difficult, or so I thought.

Year one, I dropped the class because I did poorly on the midterm and probably was not going to make the final curve; year eight (yes, it took eight years for me to give the class another try), the class was so fast paced and overwhelming I couldn't keep up due to my work and sister-parenting schedule; year nine, my final exam did not make the curve, and I failed the class (the first class I've ever failed); and year ten, I approached the class differently by giving myself more time in the day to do dozens of practice problems, talking through problems with my professor, and finding a study partner.

After all that, I finally passed! It took ten years to figure out strategies. Talk about simplicity.

Daniella Whyte, psychology researcher and writer of Life Hacks' "21 Reasons Why We Complicate Life," shares many reasons why we make life complex (Whyte, 2020). Four reasons hit home the most:

1. We seek approval and affirmation from others.
2. We compare ourselves to others.
3. We participate in drama.
4. We don't nurture our relationships.

Imagine if I had done everything I did on my fourth attempt to pass organic chemistry on my first? I would have saved ten years of my life. Don't be like me; if you are like me, sprint back to the basics, use your resources, and commit to a single goal...one strategic step at a time. KISS! Keep it simple and straightforward!

MOMENT OF REFLECTION:
"More often than not, the secret of success lies in the very basic the very small wins. The small, consistent and disciplined steps lead to big successes."

—ABHISHEK RATNA

WEEKLY TO-DO:

Think of the most complicated thing you are trying to accomplish. Take twenty minutes this week to explain your complication to a young person who you know. Young people have learned the art of simple language to understand complex concepts. When you feel the urge to give up because they don't "get it," do not. Help them understand what you are *trying to say* and answer their questions without frustration. When you have reached a comfortable threshold in explaining your complication, find another ten minutes to reflect on your conversation and write, draw, or map out the key takeaways.

WEEK 44

THE TIDE IS TURNING

"Doing the best at this moment puts you in the best place for the next moment."

—OPRAH WINFREY

Imagine lying on the beach. Beautiful white sand, palm trees lightly waving in the wind, and the ocean waves calmly gracing the shoreline. This is the vacation you've been dreaming of.

Not only did you dream of this vacation, but you also meticulously planned the details of it. Your attire is beach-ready, and you saved more than enough to enjoy a vacation of a lifetime. You feel incredible!

Now apply this feeling to your everyday life. While the perfect beach vacation is a great outcome of your planning, the process it took to get this outcome is what's important. You've done the research, shopped for the tools, found resources, and mentally prepared for a smooth sailing life experience.

The education you've received, money you've earned, networks you've built, and opportunities you've created have prepared you for the life you want and deserve. Your next steps are figuring out how to make what you've worked so hard for truly work for you.

Melissa Butler, founder of cosmetic brand The Lip Bar, is an incredible model of how the tide turns in your favor if you prepare for it. In her September 2018 TedxDetroit talk, she mentioned she always wanted to do something entrepreneurial but wasn't quite sure what to do. Graduating from college with a degree in finance and experience working on Wall Street, she compiled the tools and resources to prepare for what came next.

After years of not finding affordable vegan lipsticks in colors she wanted, she decided to develop her own. The unforgiving beauty industry was notorious for fitting "beauty" into a specific box or category that she did not fit; as a result, she created a beauty line for herself and women who also did not fit the standard—typically darker, brown-skinned women.

Even though she was harshly turned away by *Shark Tank*, an American business reality TV series, Melissa's exposure to the world was a game changer. Her tide turned into not only a multi-million-dollar company, but also an organization that advocates for women, particularly women of color.

While you may be unsure of your next steps, remember to trust that you have been building toward your future from the very beginning. Your tide is turning too, and your time has come. Now let's continue to pack your suitcases, choosing all the things you're going to need to live a fulfilled life. Don't forget to save me a spot with a view!

MOMENT OF REFLECTION:
"Preparation time is never wasted time."
—ANONYMOUS

WEEKLY TO-DO:
Take thirty minutes this week to consider all the ways that you prepare for trips, talks, class, and more. What aspects do you prioritize over others? What are your "must haves?" Draw the parallel of these momentary "must haves" to the must haves you want for your life. Consider how you'll begin to plan your present and future life accordingly.

WEEK 45

YOUR MOMENT IS NOW

"If you had one shot, or one opportunity to seize everything you ever wanted in one moment, would you capture it, or just let it slip?"

—EMINEM

Once I received rejection letters from all the US-based medical schools I applied to. The common responses were, "You should consider reapplying to medical school next year" and "You won't get a residency position when you graduate, so you probably shouldn't go to a school outside the US." When I received my second medical college admissions test (MCAT) score, I almost did not apply to medical school for that year out of fear *and* because I'd be applying in the middle of a global pandemic when school admissions requirements were ambiguous.

Coincidentally, at the same time I was reconsidering applying to medical school, I was also reading former US President Barack Obama's book, *The Promised Land.* (Obama, 2020) What resonated with me were the details behind why and when he decided to run for president in the 2008 presidential election. Obama's story inspired me to move forward with my medical school applications.

President Obama shared he had no obvious intentions of running for president until a few months leading to his official announcement. In short, members of the Democratic Party believed that considering the climate of the country, an earnest desire for change in America, Obama would be the best candidate to run. He was told that if he did not run, the opportunity the current time and climate presented may not come back around for a very long time.

As a first term US Senator who was new to Washington, DC, backing down from the opportunity would have been understandable. But after several conversations and a lot of research, he decided to give it a shot...and he won. Not only did he lean into the moment presented to him, but he also became the first Black president in the United States of America, causing celebrations around the world.

President Obama listened carefully and strategically to people he trusted around him. He took their advice and opinions seriously. He took on the challenge though he was perceived as the candidate with the least experience in Washington, DC. President Obama committed by throwing himself into his campaign with honesty and sincerity, and he had a successful outcome. Now imagine *you* leaning into a moment ripe for *you*.

I reached out to friends who have attended medical schools to which I applied, including international medical schools.

Of the international medical graduates, there were two surgery residents, a pediatric resident, a chief family medicine resident, a renowned geriatrician, and a cardiology fellow, all of whom encouraged me to apply to their respective schools as I was the ideal candidate for admissions.

After doing my research, I applied to the international medical schools, and I was admitted to all. I received competitive scholarships, and I couldn't be more grateful for leaning into the moment and taking my friends' recommendations seriously.

I believe we miss every opportunity for successful outcomes by not strategically agreeing to embrace the moment. A wise person once told me that time is going to pass by regardless of if I try an opportunity or not, and I will "miss 100 percent of the shots I don't take." (Brown, 2014)

Whenever you are given an opportunity to do something meaningful, give it serious consideration. Do your research, talk to people closest to you, but do not just say no because at the mention of it the opportunity sounds unappealing, or out of your depth. Simply say, "Thank you for the opportunity. Can I get back to you by Friday, please?" The last thing you'd want is to regret not taking the opportunity when it was handed to you.

Please do not miss any more blessings! Trying something new can be scary but taking that leap of faith may be the moment that completely transforms your life and the lives of those you love. Every chance does not always come back around.

With that said...*your* time is now. Take that leap while it's still available. Regardless of where the journey takes you, you will have learned so much along the way, and "home" will be where you left it when you return.

MOMENT OF REFLECTION:
"*Stop acting as if life is a rehearsal. Live this day as if it were your last. The past is over and gone. The future is not guaranteed.*"
—WAYNE DYER

WEEKLY TO-DO:
Decide which opportunity you are going to take this week. Talk to at least two people about it, take some time to do your research, and then begin!

WEEK 46

THE JOURNEY HAS JUST BEGUN

"Don't limit yourself. Many people limit themselves to what they think they can do. You can go as far as your mind lets you. What you believe, remember, you can achieve."

—MARY KAY ASH

You did it! You accomplished one of your goals. I hope you are reaping the benefits of your incredible efforts. Now that you have achieved the *impossible,* where do you go from here?

At this point, there is no limit to what you can accomplish. You have broken through your own glass ceiling. But you may also be exhausted and hesitant to begin the grind again. I do not blame you. Yet, it doesn't hurt to start dreaming again.

The Oxford Dictionary defines "milestone" as "an action or event marking a significant change or stage in development." Your life will be forever changed because of your accomplishments, and this change has situated you to consider the next great thing you can do. It's like earning your first $100,000 (if this is you, teach me your ways...seriously).

Once you reach a milestone, take a moment to enjoy it and relish in the moment before making your next move. You should be proud of your achievement, even if you think you still have a ways to go.

Self-made millionaire Paul Scolardi mentions in his interview with *Business Insider* that "most people don't think that far ahead," referring to people who finally reach their goal. Whenever he felt like he "made it," he knew the truth—the work wasn't actually done. He created a business to educate people on the steps he took in the stock market. He anchored his success in a greater purpose, which opened doors for him to help others and continue on a successful path.

Most of us don't know what our next steps will be as we spent so much time with our eyes on reaching this goal. Yes, there is some uncertainty about how our new "status" will affect our future, or what doors it may open. If you use your achievement to extend a greater reach, whether into communities, through teaching, or through mentorship, your journey will take you even farther. This is your greater goal.

MOMENT OF REFLECTION:
"*Where there is a will, there is a way. If there is a chance in a million that you can do something, anything, to keep what you want from ending, do it. Pry the door open or, if need be, wedge your foot in that door and keep it open.*"

—PAULINE KAEL

WEEKLY TO-DO:

Find your comfortable thinking place and spend sixty minutes this week planning your next milestone. You have already planned for and accomplished the "impossible," so you know to commit and stick to your goal. Be bold in whatever you aim to do next.

WEEK 47

SEASONS GREETINGS

"When the winds of change blow, remember...sometimes what appears dead is simply preparing for a new season."
—JANE LEE LOGAN

I grew up in Connecticut, a small state in the northeast where we experience all four seasons—winter, fall, spring, and summer. The beauty of having all seasons are the physical transitions to the landscapes.

When the colors of the leaves start to transition from green to shades of orange, red, and yellow, or when the weather becomes a bit rainier than expected, or the temperature just drops out of nowhere and specks of snow fall from the sky, or the blossoming bright flowers and green pastures start to spring out of nowhere, I know that a new season is on the horizon—and it is quite the sight to see.

Every season comes with different types of "feels." With every transition, you have to ask yourself a series of questions: Is it hot enough to wear my bathing suit to the beach? Should

I take the snow boots out of storage? Is my head in a good place to enjoy what the season will bring?

For some, seasonal transitions come with thoughts and memories. Regardless of whether your thoughts, memories, and/or events are positive or negative, we have the assurance that in a few short months, the season will shift again, leaving much behind us in the process.

When you think about it, life experiences shift in a similar way the seasons do. It's like when autumn is already here, and we have an unseasonably warm day, these signs and circumstances signal a shift in our lives that we weren't anticipating so…or so late.

When do we recognize those signals? When do we observe the changes? When do we feel confident enough to let go of one season and enter the next? Bruce Feiler, author of the *New York Times* column "This Life" and book *Life Is in the Transitions: Mastering Change at Any Age*, suggests five tips for managing life transitions.

START WITH YOUR TRANSITION SUPERPOWER.
Gravitate toward one of three phases of transitions: "the long goodbye," in which you mourn the old you; "the messy middle," in which you shed habits and create new ones; and "the new beginning," in which you unveil your fresh self." (Feiler, 2020)

IDENTIFY YOUR EMOTIONS.
Figure out what your greatest emotion is. Feiler found that 80 percent of people who he researched said that they turned to ritualistic gestures, such as singing, skydiving, or getting tattooed. Such gestures symbolize long goodbyes to ourselves and others and show we have changed and are ready for life's next phase. (Feiler, 2020)

SHED SOMETHING.
"Shedding is a way to clear out some unwanted parts of our lives to make way for the new parts to come." When we have arrived at the "messy middle," we let go of many things such as bad habits, routines, or dreams. (Feiler, 2020)

TRY SOMETHING CREATIVE.
In moments of the greatest chaos, many people turn to being creative. From cooking to diary entries, "What people seem to crave from these acts is what creation has represented since the dawn of time: a fresh start." (Feiler, 2020)

REWRITE YOUR LIFE STORY.
We control the stories we tell about our transitions. According to Feiler, "A life transition is fundamentally a meaning-making exercise. It is an autobiographical occasion, in which we are called on to revise and retell our life stories." (Feiler, 2020)

To acknowledge the changing seasons is to let go of one season before fully embracing the next. This type of transition speaks to almost every aspect in our constantly evolving lives, whether you are transitioning into a new job, a new mindset, or a relationship. Feiler states that "we must choose to take the steps and go through the process of turning our fear and anxiety into renewal and growth." (Feiler, 2020)

Letting go of things no longer serving us is challenging, but it will open space for new gifts of comfort, peace, and newness. In the same way that leaves fall off trees at the end of autumn, the tree sheds its leaves to make room for the beautiful spring season two seasons ahead.

As you begin to change, measure where you are in the moment. Whether the next moment greets you with change or maintains the status quo, and whether you are skeptical of this transition or not, there is something promising on the horizon.

Are you ready to leap off the precipice without looking, or stay put and hibernate for a while? Whatever season you are in, embrace it. Whatever transition you are approaching, celebrate it.

MOMENT OF REFLECTION:
"Spring passes and one remembers one's innocence. Summer passes and one remembers one's exuberance. Autumn passes and one remembers one's reverence. Winter passes and one remembers one's perseverance."

—YOKO ONO

WEEKLY TO-DO:

Just like the shifts of the seasons, our lives shift as well. Are you experiencing a life shift right now, and if so what "season" are you in? Are you in the building season? Are you in the manifesting season? Close your eyes and envision your life in your next season, then write down or draw two vivid images, scenes, or plans you saw. With what you wrote down or drew, consider how you will maximize your ability to grow in this season.

WEEK 48

EVERYTHING THAT GLITTERS

"I can't say I wasn't hoping for it, but I didn't see it coming."
—JESSI KIRBY, GOLDEN

"Everything that glitters ain't gold," my mother would exclaim without missing a beat.

As a teen, my requests for the latest trendy fashion or shiny devices were often met with a speech about how everything that looks great isn't as glamorous as it seems. I'm sure I gave her the "seriously?" look, but I wouldn't dare challenge her on the topic. All things trendy were a no-go.

Then, and sometimes now, I was influenced by instant gratification and felt like I needed to have what others were enjoying—that could be a boyfriend, the most recent iPhone, a purse, the Longchamp tote when I was in college, or fashionable spectacles.

When I find myself impulsive for something nowadays, I pause. I ask myself, "Do I really need this right now?" When it comes to online purchases, I take the advice of a wise loved one: Put the item(s) in the shopping cart and come back to it in three days. If the item no longer pulls at my heartstrings, delete the item, and close out the tab.

If it's a job opportunity, I revisit my three-year plan and thoughtfully determine if it will propel me toward my goals, even if the opportunity has competitive pay.

When considering an academic program, I'd consider if the program aligns with my dreams and goals, and if the expense will be worth it. Many options will present themselves as great opportunities with incredible experiences, but will the outcome fare as expected? Because you are likely to go through a lengthy application or interview process for most programs, you want to make sure that it's worth the effort.

Anything worth having requires introspection. Whether it's a purchase or deciding on an opportunity, knowing that you made the right decision is not always easy. In her December 2018 blog post, Mel Robbins provides five tools that can help you make better decisions and fewer challenges:

- **Tune into your body wisdom.** If you are choosing among different options, think about how it makes you feel. Your body will tell you if something feels right or wrong. Robbins suggests, "When you have an important decision to make, get quiet and listen." (Robbins, 2018)
- **Decisions aren't always made with just intuition, however.** Take both a rational and intuitive approach when

making big decisions. Even if you feel really good about something, take a breath and "make room for Buzz Kill." Ask yourself practical questions about the opportunity so that you can make an informed decision. (Robbins, 2018)

- **Imagine worst-case scenarios.** "Listing out as many imagined worst cases for any big decision will remove fear of the unknown, making those potential disasters loom less large in your head." (Robbins, 2018)
- **Think Positive.** Having a positive mindset when making a decision works! Focusing on what you *can* control, such as your thoughts and actions, makes it easier to focus less on the hurdles and instead what is going well. (Robbins, 2018)
- **Reflect.** After you decide, take a few minutes to ask yourself what you learned and what you would do better next time. (Robbins, 2018)

MOMENT OF REFLECTION:

"We're wired to expect the world to be brighter and more meaningful and more obviously interesting than it actually is. And when we realize that it isn't, we start looking around for the real world."

—*LEV GROSSMAN*

WEEKLY TO-DO:

Are you currently experiencing the "unexpected?" Take twenty minutes today or this weekend and reflect on how your experience is faring for you. Challenge yourself to answer this question: "Because of this experience, I want to...." Then write down your answer, your reason why, and what your choice(s) moving forward will be as a result.

WEEK 49

PERSISTENCE IS KEY

"You may encounter many defeats, but you must not be defeated. In fact, it may be necessary to encounter the defeats, so you can know who you are, what you can rise from, how you can still come out of it."

—MAYA ANGELOU

Remember the story "The Tortoise and the Hare?" As slow as the tortoise was, the boastfulness of the hare resulted in the tortoise winning the race. The tortoise wasn't overly confident compared to the hare, and it had nothing to prove. Though the fable reveals many lessons, the one that rose to the top and the one most remembered is, "Slow but steady wins the race." This moral of Aesop's fable reminds us that consistency and strategic effort lead to success. (Orlando, 1986)

The hare jumped into the race so quickly and over-confidently that it failed to understand the implications of its decisions, know who it was up against, and recognize all that was expected of him in the race—in other words, simply being the quickest to the finish line was not enough.

Success takes effort, but most importantly, consistency. We have been conditioned to want things *fast*. Whether it's food, a degree, weight loss, or more money, immediate results and instant gratification appease us. Research, such as the Marshmallow Experiment and follow up studies, show the ability to delay gratification was critical for success by investigating attentional and cognitive mechanisms with children. (Mischel et al., 1972)

Like the tortoise in "The Tortoise and the Hare," completing small steps toward a bigger goal allows time and mental space to understand what you've gotten yourself into. Smaller, gradual steps can give you a better idea of what to expect in the near future, and a greater appreciation for your accomplishment. Learning and growing *with* the process toward success helps us find better and more efficient means to become successful and to *stay* successful.

In the words of a wise loved one, "Whatever is worth having is worth fighting for." Just keep moving forward—in Ralph Waldo Emerson's words rephrased, it's about the journey, not the destination. (Goodreads, 2021)

MOMENT OF REFLECTION:
"We are what we repeatedly do. Excellence, then, is not an act, but a habit."

—*ARISTOTLE*

WEEKLY TO-DO:

Use today to decide on a task that you want to complete over the next seven days (for example, waking 20,000 steps in seven days, reading ten pages per night, etc.). Setting daily goals slowly and consistently get us to the finish line. Starting tomorrow, choose a time in your day to complete these tasks. Don't give up! You got this!

WEEK 50

GO WHERE OTHERS WILL NOT

"Look for chances to take the less-traveled roads. There are no wrong turns."

—SUSAN MAGSAMEN

There is a faraway land you've had your eyes set on for quite some time. The opportunity looks so incredible you can't stop thinking about it. The path is so green and beautiful that every time you fall asleep you can only dream of lying in the meadow looking up at the clear blue sky.

Why haven't you set out on your journey yet? *Yes, I said "yet."*

You have the map in your hands, but the road to your destination isn't clear and you don't know which path will get you there the fastest and easiest. Even if you don't have a known example of someone who has taken the path you're imagining, go anyway!

It is comfortable to remain in spaces that are familiar, which is one of the main reasons why people sometimes find it hard to take the less traveled unfamiliar road. It is time for you to chart a new path.

Steve Jobs, the late American inventor and co-founder of Apple Computer, charted an unfamiliar journey before developing the iconic Apple computer and devices. (Biography.com, 2021; The Economic Times, 2011) Early in his career, Jobs traveled to India to find enlightenment.

His time in India gave him a renewed perspective about the true cost of items, the strength behind simplicity, and being a good person. When Jobs returned home to the US, he co-founded Apple with his friend Steve Wozniak. (The Economic Times, 2011)

You may not need to travel abroad to find enlightenment as Jobs did, but you can certainly chart your own path too.

So, whatever you dream of when you close your eyes, come up with a plan to get there. Create a timeline. Figure out what the financial requirements are. Consider how the move will change your life—your career, spiritual self, or your mental health.

Time doesn't wait for anyone. If you want to seize your opportunity because it's at the forefront of your heart or mind, I challenge you to go for it with confidence, boldness, and assurance it's going to be great.

MOMENT OF REFLECTION:

"Man cannot discover new oceans unless he has the courage to lose sight of the shore."

—ANDRE GIDE

WEEKLY TO-DO:

What road have you taken that people around you have not? What did you learn or pick up along the way? Whether you have taken a different or the same road, take thirty minutes to think about something you've always wanted to do that is not conventional or an interest of others in your circle.

WEEK 51

PISS THEM OFF

"You can't let the fear of what people might say or think stop you from doing what you want to do, or else we would never do anything."

—JENNIFER LOPEZ

Going after something in a way that seems unorthodox can feel a bit scary. We as humans crave acceptance, and our heading into unknown territory takes guts. Because it's unorthodox, you may receive discouragement from others most likely because it doesn't make sense to them.

"Unorthodox" is my middle name. I had recently finished graduate school when I decided to take custody and guardianship of my youngest brother. I had this grand plan that I would work to save as much money as possible and within a year or two I would resume my pre-medical studies.

I was twenty-three years old with huge ambitions of becoming a doctor and traveling the world. I had no biological children of my own, so my responsibilities were minimal.

My mentors were particularly unaware of how the very notion of traveling abroad and "living out my twenties" was unorthodox to my family and to people where I grew up. As a first-generation college graduate, I had grown up thinking that working and caring for my family was primary.

Thus, while I had dreams that were fully supported by my loved ones, when the moment came to raise my brother, I felt that regardless of my circumstances and desire to live my best life, it was my responsibility as his older sister to help.

"Why would you do something like this?" was the first question I received from a mentor. I also received many comments from others: "He's not your child." "This is his parents' responsibility," "You're never going to become a doctor," "You're going to raise him, and you're going to forget about your dream." All these statements infuriated me.

In my "unorthodox" fashion, I chose to do what everyone was trying to convince me not to do. Not only did I do it in good faith, knowing I was the only person who seemed to believe in myself at the time, but I also knew I would be able to provide the life he deserved—a life of stability and in the arms of his family.

With this, I had something to prove. I wanted my loved ones to know that even with the sudden difficulties of raising a child, I made a commitment to myself I was going to accomplish the things I set out to accomplish. I also wanted to show them that just because someone chooses to do something in a way no one has ever seen done successfully doesn't mean I was not capable of doing it.

If you have found yourself at a crossroads, I challenge you to do whatever you believe is the best thing to do even when it pisses off the people who support you the most.

There's a lesson you'll learn when you take the unknown path, but the best-case scenario is that everything will turn out perfectly fine. You'll be so proud of what you've done.

I am incredibly proud of the young man my brother has become, and I wouldn't change my decision if the clock were turned back. I am excited to see what his future holds while building my future too. Raising my brother has made me more focused and grounded in my ambitions and stepping up in this way for him prepared me to take on medical school.

You should not stop living and reaching for your dreams. Life may be put on hold for a little while, but my map was frequently being updated. Amid it all, I met my handsome and kind husband, I've excelled in my profession, and I've worked and travelled abroad. So much for losing out on my twenties.

Sometimes it takes pissing people off to remind them what you are capable of. Go do your thing!

MOMENT OF REFLECTION:
"The folks who go after grand challenges are impatient. They're pissed off. They're sick and tired, but in a passionate way. They're driven by a fire in their bellies to make a difference."
—PETER DIAMANDIS

WEEKLY TO-DO:

Challenge yourself to do something that you've been wanting to do for a while, yet afraid that others will judge you. As long as the decision brings you happiness and pride (and is safe, legal, and does not harm others), go for it!

WEEK 52

LET'S WIN, TOGETHER

"Encourage, lift and strengthen one another. For the positive energy spread to one will be felt by us all. For we are connected, one and all."

—DEBORAH DAY

I hope that these fifty-two entries have inspired you to take control of your life, and you are motivated to move forward with what you've planned because *you* want to.

I'm going to be honest; I wrote this entry in tears.

I am overwhelmed with joy when I think of the invaluable support I've received from amazing people such as you. It is affirming to know others are on their way to accomplishing their dreams too. I truly believe we improve the success of our goals when we commit to accomplishing them together, and together we can share affirmations along the way. I have greatly benefited from mutual affirmations, so much so that the inspiration for this book came about.

Before I started on my book writing journey, I focused on #ClaimYourWorthWednesday. #ClaimYourWorthWednesday was a weekly affirmation post on social media that I created to hold myself accountable to my dreams. The goal was to figure out a way I could document my journey, and by posting every week, everyone in my world would know what paths I was on. They would know what I have committed my time and my resources to, and I could not let them, or myself, down. If I chose not to follow through for any given reason, people asked me why I was giving up, or they would remind me of my truth I had spoken of. Through my weekly expressions, they knew my purpose and what I lived for.

When people reach out to me for advice, help, or information on any platform, whether online or on the street, I am always incredibly moved. It's overwhelming to think that something I say or insight that I offer may change someone's life. I am in awe you are reading this right now. We are both motivating each other through this text and holding each other accountable.

To inspire others and ourselves, we have a lot of work to do. I want us to join forces to move this world forward. I believe all of us are called to *pay it forward*, as defined by Habitat for Humanity to "repay a kindness received with a good deed to someone else." (Habitat for Humanity, 2021)

MOMENT OF REFLECTION:

"I am only one, but still, I am one. I cannot do everything, but still, I can do something; and because I cannot do everything, I will not refuse to do something I can do."

—EDWARD EVERETT HALE

WEEKLY TO-DO:

I invite you to comment on a post or provide feedback, advice, or your thoughts where you think you can positively contribute. Do not hesitate if you feel an urge to respond; just be sure to do so out of love and respect. If there is nothing to respond to, post your own question or thoughts. Take the advice and feedback as you see fit and use what you can unashamedly.

CONCLUSION

―

"Do you plan to be a career pre-med for the rest of your life?"

This question from my mentor took my mind for a spin as I tried to find justifiable reasons why I still wasn't in medical school.

After an incredible opening session of a conference I had planned for a year, the keynote speaker, who also happened to be one of my mentors, treated me to lunch. She congratulated me on a well-planned event, wished me well on the remainder of the conference, and shared her excitement about learning more about my short-term life goals. Knowing I was still interested in medical school, as I was still completing coursework to be able to apply, she asked me the question that inspired the urgency of focusing on myself.

From raising my brother, working full-time, slowly finishing my pre-medical courses, to serving as a leader for the Student National Medical Association and more, I told her my reasons. She then went on a very powerful, heartfelt, and well-meaning speech about prioritizing yourself first so you can eventually prioritize others later in more effective and life-changing ways.

I share this story to remind you that every now and then, a little bit of inspiration can be the lightbulb that changes your life. It can change the trajectory of where you're going, whether it is with school, your family, or accomplishing the dream you always wanted to accomplish. Inspiration can go so deep into our souls. It can resonate in our brains for a while, but it can also be that boost forward we all need—certainly what I needed.

Over the last fifty-two weeks, you've had the opportunity to journey with me into your past, your present, and your future. I hope you took moments to ask yourself, "Why am I doing what I'm doing right now?" "How did I get here?" and "What has influenced me to get to this point?" The weekly to-dos helped you take practical and real-time steps to making the very best out of your goals. You have put plans and strategies in place to truly make your future happen.

Your future is promising. I want you to hold onto this book as a source and proof that you are going to get to wherever you want to go if you haven't already reached it. *Claim Your Worth Now* is the guide to make sure that you go into your future confidently and boldly.

Over ten billion dollars a year are spent on self-help books because everyone is trying to create the best versions of themselves. We're all in this boat together, but for us to get there, we have to embrace the resources within our reach. Thankfully, you have *Claim Your Worth Now* as one of them. Feel free to pick this guide up when you need encouragement to keep moving forward.

Claim Your Worth Now makes sure we all recognize that we have the strength and power within us to move our lives forward. Now you have read this book, I know you will accomplish your dreams and whatever you set out to do. Believe it or not, I have reread each week myself for motivation and inspiration.

I wrote this book for both you and me. I am confident this book is our fuel; it will ignite more dreams, more exciting adventures, and more lessons. Who knows where you will go! So, when you come up against a tough moment in your life, look back at a chapter for that extra boost of confidence.

You may have gotten to the end of this book, but it is only the beginning of your journey toward a purpose-driven and fulfilled life. If you feel like you still need more pep in your step or an extra dose of inspiration, I dare you to reread this book *again* from the beginning. Make sure you claim your worth and do whatever it takes to conquer your dreams. I am rooting for you!

ACKNOWLEDGMENTS

Writing *Claim Your Worth Now* was a journey of love, pride, and appreciation. I've discovered along my journey that publishing a book takes a village, and I am so grateful for all the support. Fulfilling this dream would not have been possible without you.

First and foremost, I'd like to thank my husband, Ademar, for supporting my crazy idea to take my affirmations for #ClaimYourWorthWednesday from Instagram and to repurpose them into a book, all while applying to medical school. I can't imagine what *Claim Your Worth Now* would be without our midnight conversations about daring to be great and chasing our dreams.

Thank you to my family, especially my mom and my dad, Deborah and Todd, for supporting me every step of the way, always. To my brothers Jonathan, Clarence, Robert, and Todd, I can't thank you enough for bearing with my lessons, challenges, and strong encouragement as I reflected on our journeys together while writing this book.

Thank you to my unrelenting friends for always having my back and holding me accountable to my new ventures. Special thanks to Tawana, Andrew, India, Javid, and Vince for allowing me to share my joys and frustrations during my writing process. Thank you for rooting for me and for *Claim Your Worth Now*.

Thank you to my mentors for inspiring and supporting me. To Mrs. Karches, Dr. Gaines, Dr. Mpasi, and Dr. Mullen, your support and advice are unmatched, and I am incredibly grateful for everything you do.

To my Georgetown University family, what an honor to have had your support along my many journeys, especially while writing this book.

Thank you to New Degree Press, Eric Koester, my outstanding editors, and all who played a role in the creation and publication of *Claim Your Worth Now*. To Rachel and Alayna, what a journey! Thank you both from the depths of my heart.

And thank you to everyone who: gave me their time for a personal interview, pre-ordered the e-book, paperback, and multiple copies to make publishing possible, helped spread the word about *Claim Your Worth Now* to gather amazing momentum, and help me publish a book I am proud of. I am sincerely grateful for all your help.

Abigail Johnson	Airelle Smith
Ademar do Nascimento	Alberto Camacho Rojas
Adriana Crawford	Alex Guyton
Adriane Saunders	Alma McKune

Aloysia Jean
Andrew Street
Andria Wisler
Antoinette Leonard-Jean Charles
April Jonhson
Arielle Thornton
Brittany Gore
Carlene Fonseca
Calvin Willoughby
Chandni Patel
Chariss Cox
Charlene Brown-McKenzie
Christine Edwards
Clarence Fuller III
Cynthia Robinson
D'Sena' Warren
Danny Burke
DeJoire' Hall
Dennikeya Randolph
Derrick Green
Deven Comen
Devita Bishundat
Dominique Jordan
Donnae Thomas
Ebony Johnson
Edna Foster
Ellie Nyakīo Hunja
Emilio Mendez
Eric Koester
Erika Costa-Salvador
Ernesha Webb Mazinyo

Ferne Barrow
Francine Rubio
Fred Stennis
Hazael Ajayi
Heidi Elmendorf
Holly Dancy
Ianthe Metzger
Ijeoma Njaka
India Williams
Jackie Gray
Jacqueline Blake
Jarvis Matthews
Jasmine Morton
Javid Buchanan
Jeff Williams
JeriI Clinch
Jessica Galvan
Jonathan Young
Joseph Johnson
Kandace Whaley
Kareen Currey
Katharine Blankman
Katherine Harripersaud
Kelly Winter
Keshia Butts
Keshia Woods
Kesslyn Brade-Stennis
Keytoria Jenkins
Khadijah Brydson-Van
Kirsty Fontaine
Kristen Street
Kristin Watson

Ksean Henderson
LaNysha Foss
LaRhonda Leslie
Leya Abebe
Linda Allen
Loneisha Mabry
Mark Joy
Matthew D. Lewis
Melissa Foy
Michael J.A. Davis
Michelle Paulishen
Michelle V. Thomas
Milyanny Calo
Minnie Annan
Molly Morrison
Monalisa Domingoz
Monika Khan
Nana Yaw Adu-Sarkodie
Nardos Ghebreab
Nicole Friday
Nicole McKenzie
Nikia Wilkins
Nkiruka Ogbuchiekwe
Noah Martin
Olga Gromadzka
Olivia Madison
Patricia Deans
Vincent Dixon

Paulette Trimble
Priscilla Mpasi
Rashonda Ward
Raycean Wright Osborn
Regina Coleman
Renee King
Robert Jackson III
Robert Young
Robin Williams
Roosevelt Young
Sanessa Griffiths
Scott Fleming
Shanell Jefferson
Shannon Mooney
Shay Edwards
Sherine Powerful
Susan Karches
Susannah McGowan
Tamara Moore
Tanay Moore
Tawana McClure
Tayvia Pierce
Todd Wallace Sr.
Tyeese L. Gaines
Tyra Gross
Victoria Gross

APPENDIX

INTRODUCTION

Benner, Dana. "The Wages of War." HistoryNet, November 12, 2020. https://www.historynet.com/the-wages-of-war.htm.

LaRosa, John. "The $10 Billion Self-Improvement Market Adjusts to a New Generation." Market Research Blog, October 11, 2018. https://blog.marketresearch.com/the-10-billion-self-improvement-market-adjusts-to-new-generation#:~:text=The%20total%20US%20self%2Dimprovement,infomercials%20and%20commercial%20diet%20programs.

MarieTV. "Dr. Tererai Trent: How to Achieve Your "Impossible" Dreams." March 4, 2019. Video, 39:48. www.youtube.com/watch?v=Ewh1zT8VpQo.

WEEK 1

"Denis Waitley Quotes." BrainyQuote. Accessed May 19, 2021. https://www.brainyquote.com/quotes/denis_waitley_125740.

"Thomas A. Edison Quotes." BrainyQuote. Accessed May 19, 2021. https://www.brainyquote.com/quotes/thomas_a_edison_132683.

Vaden, Rory. Take the Stairs: 7 Steps to Achieving True Success. Perigee/Penguin, 2013.

WEEK 2

MarieTV. "Dr. Tererai Trent: How to Achieve Your "Impossible" Dreams." March 4, 2019. Video, 39:48. www.youtube.com/watch?v=Ewh1zT8VpQo.

WEEK 3

BET Networks. "Taraji P. Henson Speaks on Typecasting—BET Breaks." September 13, 2017. Video, 1:07. https://www.youtube.com/watch?v=hjbUU8_ip3Q.

Henson, Taraji P. Around the Way Girl: A Memoir. New York, NY: Simon & Schuster, 2016.

Juma, Norbert. "155 Maya Angelou Quotes Celebrating Success, Love & Life." Everyday Power, April 13, 2021. https://everydaypower.com/maya-angelou-quotes/.

WEEK 4

Davis, Rachaell. "Denzel Washington Salutes Black Actresses in Empowering NAACP Awards Speech." Essence, February 12, 2017. https://www.essence.com/awards-events/red-carpet/naacp-image-awards/denzel-washington-speech/.

Gupta, R., T.R. Koscik, A. Bechara, & D. Tranel. "The Amygdala and Decision-making." Neuropsychologia, 49(4), 760–766, March 2011. https://doi.org/10.1016/j.neuropsychologia.2010.09.029.

Peralta, Eyder. "Two Excerpts You Should Read from Obama's Morehouse Speech." NPR, May 19, 2013. https://www.npr.org/sections/thetwo-way/2013/05/19/185348873/two-excerpts-you-should-read-from-obamas-morehouse-speech.

WEEK 5

"A Quote by C. JoyBell C." Goodreads. Accessed May 26, 2021. https://www.goodreads.com/quotes/424700-we-can-t-be-afraid-of-change-you-may-feel-very.

"A Quote from Unapologetically You." Goodreads. Accessed May 26, 2021. https://www.goodreads.com/quotes/319475-renew-release-let-go-yesterday-s-gone-there-s-nothing-you-can.

The Oxford Pocket Dictionary of Current English. Encyclopedia.com. 18 Jun. 2021." Encyclopedia.com. https://www.encyclopedia.com/humanities/dictionaries-thesauruses-pictures-and-press-releases/grudge-0.

WEEK 6

Giroux, Melissa. "30 Best Quotes for When You Feel Like Giving Up: 2021." Nomad Life 101, May 10, 2021. https://nomadlife101.com/quotes-when-you-feel-like-giving-up/.

Lynch, Tony. "'Yesterday Is Gone...'—Mother Teresa." Keep Thinking Big, February 23, 2021. https://keepthinkingbig.com/yesterday-is-gone/.

Rahkim Sabree's instagram post on manifestation: "I wrote myself a check for $10 Million. I take that check everywhere I go. I do this as a means to consciously manifest. How are you manifesting?" (@rahkimsabree, November 5, 2020).

WEEK 7

Croft, Alyssa, Elizabeth W. Dunn, and Jordi Quoidbach. "From Tribulations to Appreciation." Social Psychological and Personality Science 5, no. 5 (2013): 511–16. https://doi.org/10.1177/1948550613512510.

Kelly-Gangi, Carol. Essential Black Wisdom: Quotes of Inspiration and Strength. New York: Fall River Press, 2018.

Mani, Ranjani. "International Women's Day – Ranjani Mani." Women In Big Data, March 8, 2021. https://www.womeninbigdata.org/ranjani_mani/.

"Metamorphosis." Dictionary.com. Accessed June 27, 2021. https://www.dictionary.com/browse/metamorphosis.

Palmiter, David, Mary Alvord, Rosalind Dorlen, Lillian Comas-Diaz, Suniya S. Luthar, Salvatore R. Maddi, H. Katherine (Kit) O'Neill, Karen W. Saakvitne, and Richard Glenn Tedeschi. "Building Your Resilience." American Psychological Association, February 1, 2020. https://www.apa.org/topics/resilience.

Young, Toddchelle. "Left On the Side of the Road." Web log. Journey Revisited (blog), 2017. https://sites.google.com/view/ty-journey-revisited/left-on-the-side-of-the-road?authuser=0.

WEEK 8

"Door of Opportunity Quotes (19 Quotes)." Goodreads. Accessed May 26, 2021. https://www.goodreads.com/quotes/tag/door-of-opportunity.

"Door Sayings and Door Quotes." Wise Sayings. Accessed May 26, 2021. https://www.wisesayings.com/door-quotes/#ixzz6jqko-9QxT.

"Organizing Your Social Sciences Research Paper: Writing a Research Proposal." Research Guides. Accessed June 9, 2021. https://libguides.usc.edu/writingguide/researchproposal.

WEEK 9

Gluck, Samantha. "Self-Help Quotes." HealthyPlace. Accessed May 27, 2021. https://www.healthyplace.com/insight/quotes/self-help-quote.

WEEK 10

"100 Dream Quotes to Inspire You and Motivate You." Gathering Dreams, October 7, 2019. https://gatheringdreams.com/dream-quotes/.

Dye, Lee. "'Hidden Truths' Are in Those Dreams." ABC News. ABC News Network, March 4, 2009. https://abcnews.go.com/Technology/DyeHard/story?id=7009297&page=1.

WEEK 11

Jackson, Sarah E., Andrew Steptoe, and Jane Wardle. "The Influence of Partner's Behavior on Health Behavior Change." JAMA Internal Medicine 175, no. 3 (2015): 385. https://doi.org/10.1001/jamainternmed.2014.7554.

Meah, Asad. "35 Inspirational Quotes on Commitment." AwakenTheGreatnessWithin, April 25, 2018. https://www.awakenthegreatnesswithin.com/35-inspirational-quotes-on-commitment/.

WEEK 12

"A quote by Elbert Hubbard." Goodreads, 2021. https://www.goodreads.com/quotes/877210-no-one-gets-very-far-unless-he-accomplishes-the-impossible.

Koufalis, G. The Dream Is Free but the Hustle Is Sold Separately. George Koufalis, 2017.

Pickard-Whitehead, G. "60 Famous Hard Work Quotes to Motivate Your Team." Small Business Trends, April 10, 2020. https://smallbiztrends.com/2019/08/famous-hard-work-quotes.html.

WEEK 13

Norbert, J. "50 Past Quotes Celebrating What You've Learned." Everyday Power, June 25, 2020. https://everydaypower.com/wise-past-quotes/.

"Top 20 Inspiring Oprah Winfrey Quotes That Will Empower You." Goalcast, August 19, 2019. https://www.goalcast.com/2016/09/28/top-20-inspiring-oprah-winfrey-quotes-that-will-empower-you/.

WEEK 14

"15: You Are Your Best Thing—The Refill with Latisha Carr." Spotify, August 7, 2019. https://open.spotify.com/episode/3i53MbT5K-1frS447qTM1Pq.

Ellis, D. "10 Warren Buffett Quotes for Your Money Mindset." PayPath, October 14, 2020. https://www.paypath.com/Personal/warren-buffett-quote.

"Stay Ready, So You Don't Have to Get Ready." Turning Managers into Leaders. Merge's Blog, October 22, 2012. http://mergeg.sg-host.com/stay-ready-so-you-dont-have-to-get-ready/

WEEK 15

"Friendships: Enrich Your Life and Improve Your Health." Mayo Clinic, August 24, 2019. https://www.mayoclinic.org/healthy-lifestyle/adult-health/in-depth/friendships/art-20044860

Williamson, Jennifer. "25 Quotes about Making New Friends (And Starting Again)." Healing Brave, March 3, 2017. https://healingbrave.com/blogs/all/quotes-making-new-friends.

WEEK 16

"Do the Hard Jobs First. The Easy Jobs Will Take Care of Themselves." Philosiblog, April 22, 2012. https://philosiblog.com/2011/05/03/352/.

Jimmy. "Hardest or Easiest Work First? What the Research Shows." The Productive Engineer, April 28, 2021. https://theproductiveengineer.net/hardest-or-easiest-work-first-what-the-research-shows/.

Tracy, Brian. Eat That Frog!: 21 Great Ways to Stop Procrastinating and Get More Done in Less Time. Williston, VT, USA: Berrett-Koehler Publishers, 2017.

Vedantam, Shankar, Thomas Lu, Angus Chen, Rhaina Cohen, and Tara Boyle. "Creatures of Habit: How Habits Shape Who We Are—And Who We Become." KUOW, December 30, 2019. https://www.kuow.org/stories/creatures-of-habit-how-habits-shape-who-we-are-and-who-we-become.

WEEK 17

Kelly-Gangi, C. Essential Black Wisdom: Quotes of Inspiration and Strength. New York: Fall River Press, 2018.

Khullar, Dhruv. "Even as the US Grows More Diverse, the Medical Profession Is Slow to Follow." The Washington Post. WP Company, September 24, 2018. https://www.washingtonpost.com/national/health-science/even-as-the-us-grows-more-diverse-the-medical-profession-is-slow-to-follow/2018/09/21/6e048d66-aba4-11e8-a8d7-0f63ab8b1370_story.html.

Lett, L.A., H.M. Murdock, W.U. Orji, J. Aysola, R. Sebro. "Trends in Racial/Ethnic Representation Among US Medical Students." JAMA Netw Open, 2019. doi:10.1001/jamanetworkopen.2019.10490.

Price, Eboni G., Neil R. Powe, David E. Kern, Sherita Hill Golden, Gary S. Wand, and Lisa A. Cooper. "Improving the Diversity Climate in Academic Medicine: Faculty Perceptions as a Catalyst for Institutional Change." Academic Medicine 84, no. 1 (2009): 95–105. https://doi.org/10.1097/acm.0b013e3181900f29.

WEEK 18

"A Quote by Elisabeth Kübler-Ross." Goodreads. Accessed June 10, 2021. https://www.goodreads.com/quotes/6826-people-are-like-stained-glass-windows-they-sparkle-and-shine-when.

Purrington. "Carl Jung: 'Who Looks Outside Dreams; Who Looks inside Awakes'." Carl Jung Depth Psychology, February 8, 2020. https://carljungdepthpsychologysite.blog/2020/02/08/carl-jung-i-am-afraid-that-the-mere-fact-of-my-presence-takes-you-away-from-yourself/#.YJR81WZKhJU.

WEEK 19

MarieTV. "Glennon Doyle Untamed: Her Marriage, Sexuality & Choosing an Authentic Life." March 9, 2020. Video, 48:02,. https://www.youtube.com/watch?v=XhOxjFaga78&t=1998s.

"Moliere Quotes." BrainyQuote. Accessed May 12, 2021. https://www.brainyquote.com/quotes/moliere_378426.

Nichols, Lisa. "No Matter What!: 9 Steps to Living the Life You Love." New York, New York, Grand Central Life & Style, 2009.

WEEK 20

Agyei, Steve. "'You Will Never Find Time for Anything. If You Want Time, You Must Make It." Medium, July 11, 2016. https://medium.com/@steveagyeibeyondlifestyle/you-will-never-find-time-for-anything-if-you-want-time-you-must-make-it-79984bf1cf24.

Clayton, Russell, Christopher Thomas, and Jack Smothers. "How to Do Walking Meetings Right." Harvard Business Review, August 05, 2015. https://hbr.org/2015/08/how-to-do-walking-meetings-right.

Festini, Sara B., Ian M. McDonough, and Denise C. Park. "The Busier the Better: Greater Busyness Is Associated with Better Cognition." Frontiers in Aging Neuroscience 8 (2016). https://doi.org/10.3389/fnagi.2016.00098.

Marelisa. "59 Time Quotes to Help You Make the Most of Your Time." Daring To Live Fully, June 17, 2016. https://daringtolivefully.com/time-quotes.

Sifferlin, Alexandra. "Brain Aging: Staying Busy Will Keep Your Brain Young." Time, May 19, 2016. https://time.com/4341680/busy-brain-cognitive-function-aging/.

WEEK 21

"A Quote from Om Chanting and Meditation." Goodreads. Accessed May 21, 2021. https://www.goodreads.com/quotes/348090-if-you-want-to-conquer-the-anxiety-of-life-live.

Becker-Phelps, Leslie. "Don't Just React: Choose Your Response." Psychology Today. Sussex Publishers. Accessed May 21, 2021. https://www.psychologytoday.com/us/blog/making-change/201307/dont-just-react-choose-your-response.

Gaines Reid, Tyeese. The Get a Life Campaign: A Pocket Guide for the Busy Woman Who Wants It All. West Conshohocken, PA: Infinity Publishing, 2007.

Mayo Clinic Staff. "A Beginner's Guide to Meditation." Mayo Foundation for Medical Education and Research. Mayo Clinic, April 22, 2020. https://www.mayoclinic.org/tests-procedures/meditation/in-depth/meditation/art-20045858.

Studio, RYOT. "Shifting Your Mindset From 'I Have To' To 'I Get To'." HuffPost, July 15, 2019. https://www.huffpost.com/entry/shifting-your-mindset-from-i-have-to-to-i-get-to_n_5d14fd4ae4b03d6116385558.

WEEK 22

Clarke, Jodi. "If You're Always Over-Scheduled, Find Out Why You Need to Slow Down." Verywell Mind, April 7, 2021. https://www.verywellmind.com/how-the-glorification-of-busyness-impacts-our-well-being-4175360.

"Iyanla Vanzant Quotes." BrainyQuote. Accessed May 21, 2021. https://www.brainyquote.com/quotes/iyanla_vanzant_519952.

"Top 13 Quotes of Claudia Black Famous Quotes and Sayings." Inspiring Quotes. Accessed May 21, 2021. https://www.inspiringquotes.us/author/7931-claudia-black.

WEEK 23

"A Quote by Confucius." Goodreads. Accessed May 21, 2021. https://www.goodreads.com/quotes/184310-the-man-who-asks-a-question-is-a-fool-for.

Bostock, Bill. "The Sinister Story of Nike's 'Just Do It' Slogan, Which Was Inspired by the Last Words of a Murderer before He Was Executed." Business Insider, August 10, 2019. https://www.businessinsider.com/nike-just-do-it-inspired-utah-killer-gary-gilmore-2019-7.

"Questioning and Posing Problems." The Institute for Habits of Mind. Accessed May 21, 2021. https://www.habitsofmindinstitute.org/resources/quotes/hom-quotes/7-questioning-posing-problems/.

Schweitzer, Maurice. "Why You Shouldn't Be Afraid to Ask Sensitive Questions." Knowledge@Wharton. Wharton School at the University of Pennsylvania, January 12, 2021. https://knowledge.wharton.upenn.edu/article/why-you-shouldnt-be-afraid-to-ask-sensitive-questions/.

WEEK 24

Kondō, Marie. Spark Joy: An Illustrated Master Class on the Art of Organizing and Tidying Up. The Life Changing Magic of Tidying Up. New York: Ten Speed Press, 2016.

Robbins, John. The New Good Life: Living Better Than Ever in an Age of Less. New York: Ballantine Books, 2010.

"You Can't Reach for Anything New if Your Hands Are Still Full of Yesterday's Junk.—Louise Smith." Quotes Pedia, July 13, 2020. https://www.quotespedia.org/authors/l/louise-smith/you-cant-reach-for-anything-new-if-your-hands-are-still-full-of-yesterdays-junk-louise-smith/.

WEEK 25

Mani, Mukesh. "36 Inspirational Quotes on Why You Should Always Put Yourself First." Outofstress.com, July 27, 2020. https://www.outofstress.com/inspirational-quotes-about-putting-yourself-first/.

WEEK 26

"A Quote from Simple Reminders." Goodreads. Accessed May 9, 2021. https://www.goodreads.com/quotes/1307115-your-calm-mind-is-the-ultimate-weapon-against-your-challenges.

"A Quote from Wouldn't Take Nothing for My Journey Now." Goodreads. Accessed May 9, 2021. https://www.goodreads.com/quotes/427696-every-person-needs-to-take-one-day-away-a-day.

"The Benefits of Taking a Mental Health Day." McLean Hospital, December 16, 2020. https://www.mcleanhospital.org/essential/benefits-taking-mental-health-day.

WEEK 27

"Arnaud Desjardins Quote: Life Is Movement. The More Life There Is, the More Flexibility There Is..." Inspiring Quotes. Accessed May 9, 2021. https://www.inspiringquotes.us/quotes/7crq_XIxtpLAk.

"Flexibility Makes Buildings to Be Stronger...—Quote." AllAuthor. Accessed May 9, 2021. https://allauthor.com/quotes/192421/.

WEEK 28

"A Quote from Lit From Within." Goodreads. Accessed May 9, 2021. https://www.goodreads.com/quotes/266296-a-simple-life-is-not-seeing-how-little-we-can.

Bilyeu, Tom. "Lisa Nichols on Rescuing Yourself, Overcoming Fear, and Finding Success by Serving Others." Inside Quest, December 31, 2016. Video, 55:14. www.youtube.com/watch?v=tSxhIp-4l1DY.

"Depression: What Is Burnout?" Institute for Quality and Efficiency in Health Care (IQWiG). InformedHealth.org. Last modified June 18, 2020. https://www.ncbi.nlm.nih.gov/books/NBK279286/.

Robbins, Anthony. "Decisions: The Pathway to Power." In Awaken the Giant Within: How to Take Immediate Control of Your Mental, Emotional, Physical and Financial, 40. United States: Simon & Schuster, 2007.

WEEK 29

Barnes, Charles A. "COMMENTARY: Fly, Run, Walk or Crawl to Advance MLK's Vision." The Courier-Post, January 12, 2018. https://www.courierpostonline.com/story/opinion/readers/2018/01/12/commentary-fly-run-walk-crawl-advance-mlks-vision/1029899001/.

"Ellen Johnson Sirleaf Quotes (Author of This Child Will Be Great)." Goodreads. Accessed May 21, 2021. https://www.goodreads.com/author/quotes/2116089.Ellen_Johnson_Sirleaf.

WEEK 30

Claris. "The Reverend Dr. Martin Luther King, Jr. at Oberlin." Oberlin College Archives, August 5, 1997. https://www2.oberlin.edu/external/EOG/BlackHistoryMonth/MLK/MLKmainpage.html.

"Toni Morrison Interviewed by Don Swaim on September 15, 1987." Don Swaim Collection. Mahn Center for Archives & Special Collections, Ohio University Libraries, September 15, 1987. https://media.library.ohio.edu/digital/collection/donswaim/id/6366/.

WEEK 31

"10 Quotes on Overcoming Obstacles That Will Motivate You." Teamphoria, July 17, 2018. https://www.teamphoria.com/10-quotes-on-overcoming-obstacles-that-will-motivate-you/.

"Famous Pablo Picasso Quotes." Pablo Picasso Quotes. Accessed May 11, 2021. https://www.pablopicasso.org/quotes.

WEEK 32

Frank, Tara Jaye. "5 Things Women Leaders Should Stop Doing. TODAY." The League of Women in Government. Last modified July 10, 2019. https://www.leagueofwomeningovernment.org/2016/02/5-things-women-leaders-should-stop-doing-today/.

Growth, Aimee. "You're the Average of the Five People You Spend the Most Time With." Business Insider. Last modified July 24, 2012. https://www.businessinsider.com/jim-rohn-youre-the-average-of-the-five-people-you-spend-the-most-time-with-2012-7#:~:text=David%20P%20Brown%20Motivational%20speaker,the%20average%20of%20all%20outcomes.

"Wilferd Peterson Quotes (Author of The Art of Living)." Goodreads. Accessed April 10, 2021. https://www.goodreads.com/author/quotes/707594.Wilferd_Peterson.

WEEK 33

"Cry Quotes (470 Quotes)." Goodreads. Accessed May 21, 2021. https://www.goodreads.com/quotes/tag/cry.

"Iyanla Vanzant Quotes." BrainyQuote. Accessed May 21, 2021. https://www.brainyquote.com/quotes/iyanla_vanzant_519947.

WEEK 34

"How to Get Out of Debt With the Debt Snowball Plan." Ramsey Solutions, March 9, 2021. https://www.daveramsey.com/blog/get-out-of-debt-with-the-debt-snowball-plan.

Hughes, Kris. "25 of the Best Planning Quotes." ProjectManager.com, August 10, 2020. https://www.projectmanager.com/blog/planning-quotes.

Singletary, Michelle. "College Degrees Don't Always Prepare Applicants for a Job. Employers Demand Them Anyway." The Washington Post, September 17, 2019. https://www.washingtonpost.com/business/economy/college-degrees-dont-always-prepare-applicants-for-a-job-employers-demand-them-anyway/2019/09/17/ffb554dc-d959-11e9-bfb1-849887369476_story.html.

WEEK 35

Harris, Ron. "Tyler Perry Christens New Studio with Help of Oprah, Others." AP NEWS. Associated Press, October 6, 2019. https://apnews.com/article/ga-state-wire-halle-berry-us-news-ap-top-news-spike-lee-61c3c9a83a384c5a8dba571196c39420.

Lee, Elise. "44 Self Love Quotes That Will Make You Mentally Stronger." Lifehack, December 23, 2019. https://www.lifehack.org/567391/frank-self-love-quotes.

Medrut, Flavia. "31 Self-Love Quotes That Are Genuinely Empowering." Goalcast, April 8, 2021. https://www.goalcast.com/2020/01/06/self-love-quotes/.

Porter, Billy, and Lacey Rose. "Billy Porter Breaks a 14-Year Silence: 'This Is What HIV-Positive Looks Like Now.'" The Hollywood Reporter, May 19, 2021. https://www.hollywoodreporter.com/news/general-news/billy-porter-hiv-positive-diagnosis-1234954742/.

WEEK 36

Godin, Seth. "The Thing about Goals." Seth's Blog, January 8, 2009. https://seths.blog/2009/01/the-thing-about/.

"Les Brown Quotes." BrainyQuote. Accessed May 11, 2021. https://www.brainyquote.com/quotes/les_brown_391112#.

Niles, Frank. "Why Goal Visualization Works." HuffPost, August 17, 2011. https://www.huffpost.com/entry/visualization-goals_b_878424.

WEEK 37

"A Quote from from the Heart." Goodreads. Accessed May 22, 2021. https://www.goodreads.com/quotes/976571-venture-outside-your-comfort-zone-to-stop-growing-is-to.

Bradberry, Travis. "8 Powerful Habits of Profoundly Influential People." Next Big Idea Club, August 4, 2017. https://nextbigideaclub.com/magazine/8-powerful-habits-profoundly-influential-people/15633/.

WEEK 38

Bueno, Antoinette. "Tabitha Brown Breaks Down Her Catchphrases and Social Media Rise." Entertainment Tonight, July 10, 2020. https://www.etonline.com/tabitha-brown-breaks-down-her-catchphrases-and-rise-to-social-media-superstardom-exclusive-149432.

Thakur, Anand. "Epictetus Quote." Minimalist Quotes, February 6, 2021. https://minimalistquotes.com/epictetus-quote-17660/.

"You Would Be Very Surprised with How Much Positive Changes That…" ReadBeach.com. Accessed May 12, 2021. https://readbeach.com/quote/you-would-be-very-surprise-with-how-much-positive-changes-that-you-cou.

WEEK 39

"A Quote from The Soul of Man Under Socialism, and Selected Critical Prose." Goodreads. Accessed May 12, 2021. https://www.goodreads.com/quotes/31784-the-public-have-an-insatiable-curiosity-to-know-everything-except.

Hammond, Claudia. "When Should You Follow Your Gut Instinct?" BBC Future. BBC, November 5, 2019. https://www.bbc.com/future/article/20191031-when-should-you-follow-your-gut-instinct.

Holt, John. Teach Your Own: The John Holt Book of Homeschooling. Hachette Books, 2009.

Martin, Gary. "'Curiosity Killed the Cat'—the Meaning and Origin of This Phrase." The Phrase Finder. Accessed June 23, 2021. https://www.phrases.org.uk/meanings/curiosity-killed-the-cat.html.

WEEK 40

"9 Health and Wellness Quotes to Inspire You." Chiro One, May 22, 2020. https://www.chiroone.com/blog/9-health-and-wellness-quotes-to-inspire-you/.

Mac, Jim, Maxime Lagacé, Shilajit, and Kevin Millet. "105 Health Quotes for a Better Mind, Body (And Life)." Wisdom Quotes, April 21, 2021. https://wisdomquotes.com/health-quotes/.

Nishat, Nayma. "The 10 Different Types of Health." The Health & Fitness Book. The World Book, March 22, 2021. https://theworldbook.org/types-of-health/.

Rosenburg, Eric, and Cara Herbert. "Why Your Financial Health Matters." Self, April 20, 2020. https://www.self.inc/blog/why-your-financial-health-important.

WEEK 41

Martinez, Nikki. "175 Love Yourself Quotes That Will Increase Your Self Esteem." Everyday Power, January 30, 2021. https://everydaypower.com/love-yourself-quotes-2/.

Youdline, Joseph. "Do 'Likes' on Social Media Affect Our Mental Health?" The Famuan, September 26, 2019. http://www.thefamuanonline.com/2019/09/26/do-likes-on-social-media-affect-our-mental-health/.

Sherman, Lauren E., Ashley A. Payton, Leanna M. Hernandez, Patricia M. Greenfield, and Mirella Dapretto. "The Power of the Like in Adolescence." Psychological Science 27, no. 7 (2016): 1027–35. https://doi.org/10.1177/0956797616645673.

WEEK 42

Lagacé, Maxime. "380 Powerful Money Quotes That Will Make You…" Wisdom Quotes, January 24, 2021. https://wisdomquotes.com/money-quotes/.

O'Shea, Bev, and Lauren Schwahn. "Budgeting 101: How to Budget Money." NerdWallet, January 13, 2021. https://www.nerdwallet.com/article/finance/how-to-budget.

WEEK 43

"Basics Quotes (12 quotes)." Goodreads. Accessed June 25, 2021. https://www.goodreads.com/quotes/tag/basics.

Becker, J. "Hans Hofmann on Minimalism." Becoming Minimalist, August 20, 2008. https://www.becomingminimalist.com/hans-hofmann-on-minimalism/.

"Software Tree—White Papers—The KISS Principles." Software Tree. Accessed June 25, 2021. http://www.softwaretree.com/v1/KISSPrinciples.html.

Whyte, D. "21 Reasons Why We Complicate Life." Lifehack, December 4, 2020. https://www.lifehack.org/387622/21-ways-complicate-life.

WEEK 44

Butler, Melissa. "Why You Think You're Ugly." Filmed September 2018 at TEDxDetroit, Detroit, MI. Video, 7:59. https://www.ted.com/talks/melissa_butler_why_you_think_you_re_ugly.

Meah, Asad. "35 Inspirational Quotes on Preparation." AwakenTheGreatnessWithin, April 1, 2018. https://www.awakenthegreatnesswithin.com/35-inspirational-quotes-on-preparation/.

WEEK 45

Brown, Paul B. "'You Miss 100% of the Shots You Don't Take.' You Need to Start Shooting at Your Goals." Forbes Magazine, January 12, 2014. https://www.forbes.com/sites/actiontrumpseverything/2014/01/12/you-miss-100-of-the-shots-you-dont-take-so-start-shooting-at-your-goal/?sh=142c74d46a40.

Obama, Barack. A Promised Land. The Presidential Memoirs, Volume 1. New York, NY: Crown Publishing Group, 2020.

"Seize The Moment Quotes." The STRIVE, February 3, 2021. https://thestrive.co/seize-the-moment-quotes/

WEEK 46

Oxford Dictionary. Definition of MILESTONE." Lexico Dictionaries | English. Accessed June 30, 2021. https://www.lexico.com/en/definition/milestone.

SUCCESS Staff. "15 Quotes to Overcome Your Self-Limiting Beliefs." SUCCESS, January 21, 2019. https://www.success.com/15-quotes-to-overcome-your-self-limiting-beliefs/.

Sweatt, Lydia. "17 Motivational Quotes to Help You Achieve Your Dreams." SUCCESS, March 2, 2021. https://www.success.com/17-motivational-quotes-to-help-you-achieve-your-dreams/.

WEEK 47

"A Quote by Yoko Ono." Goodreads. Accessed May 12, 2021. https://www.goodreads.com/quotes/23091-spring-passes-and-one-remembers-one-s-innocence-summer-passes-and.

Feiler, Bruce. "Feeling Stuck? Five Tips for Managing Life Transitions." The New York Times, July 16, 2020. https://www.nytimes.com/2020/07/16/well/mind/managing-life-transitions.html.

Slade, Thom. "The Winds of Change." IveMovedOn.com, September 13, 2020. https://ivemovedon.com/winds-change-blow-remember-sometimes-appears-dead-simply-preparing-new-season/.

WEEK 48

"A Quote from Golden." Goodreads. Accessed May 22, 2021. https://www.goodreads.com/quotes/911639-i-can-t-say-i-wasn-t-hoping-for-it-but-i.

"Lev Grossman Quote." Quote Fancy. Accessed May 22, 2021. https://quotefancy.com/quote/1217653/Lev-Grossman-We-re-wired-to-expect-the-world-to-be-brighter-and-more-meaningful-and-more.

Robbins, Mel. "How to Know You're Making the Right Decision." Mel Robbins, December 13, 2018. https://melrobbins.com/how-to-know-youre-making-the-right-decision/.

WEEK 49

"A Quote from Self-Reliance—Ralph Waldo Emerson." Goodreads. Accessed May 25, 2021. https://www.goodreads.com/quotes/859087-its-the-not-the-destination-it-s-the-journey.

Mischel, W., E.B. Ebbesen, A.R. Zeiss. Cognitive and Attentional Mechanisms in Delay of Gratification. J Pers Soc Psychol. 1972 Feb;21(2):204-18. doi: 10.1037/h0032198.

Orlando, Jo. "The Tortoise and the Hare: an Aesop Fable." Clovis, CA: Clovis Unified School District, 1986.

Schnall, Marianne. "An Interview with Maya Angelou." Psychology Today. Sussex Publishers, February 17, 2009. https://www.psychologytoday.com/us/blog/the-guest-room/200902/interview-maya-angelou.

"Thoughts on the Business of Life." Forbes Magazine. Accessed May 22, 2021. https://www.forbes.com/quotes/659/.

WEEK 50

"A Quote from The 10 Best of Everything Families." Goodreads. Accessed May 26, 2021. https://www.goodreads.com/quotes/1194053-look-for-chances-to-take-the-less-traveled-roads-there-are.

Bryant, Justin. "Man Cannot Discover New Oceans Unless He Has the Courage to Lose Sight of the Shore." Self Made Success, August 13, 2019. https://selfmadesuccess.com/man-cannot-discover-new-oceans-andre-gide-2/.

"Steve Jobs." Biography.com. A&E Networks Television, February 4, 2021. https://www.biography.com/business-figure/steve-jobs.

"Trip to India as Teen Was a Life-Changer for Steve Jobs." The Economic Times, October 7, 2011. https://economictimes.indiatimes.com/news/international/trip-to-india-as-teen-was-a-life-changer-for-steve-jobs/articleshow/10264889.cms.

WEEK 51

Buchanan, Leigh. "Big Thinkers Are Pissed Off & Passionate." Inc.com, October 31, 2012. https://www.inc.com/leigh-buchanan/

big-ideas/peter-diamandis-big-thinkers-pissed-off-and-passionate.html.

"Jennifer Lopez Quote." AZ Quotes. Accessed May 26, 2021. https://www.azquotes.com/quote/879653.

WEEK 52

"Support Sayings and Support Quotes." Wise Sayings. Accessed May 12, 2021. https://www.wisesayings.com/support-quotes/#ixzz6jN3bMjA6.

"The Meaning of Giving Back and Paying It Forward." Habitat for Humanity. Accessed May 12, 2021. https://www.habitat.org/stories/meaning-giving-back-and-paying-it-forward.